AF622956

THERESA GANZ
GRAND ILLUSION

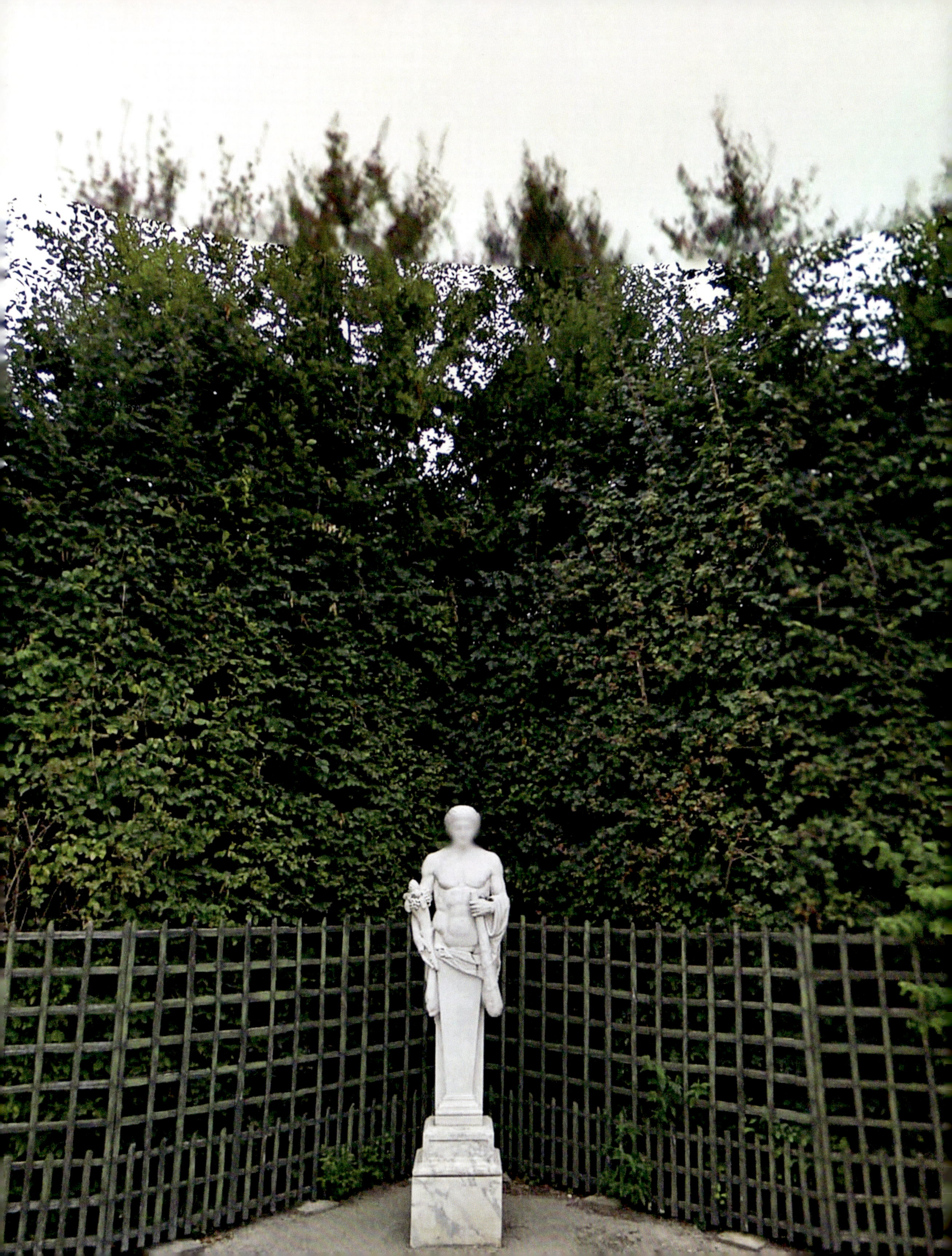

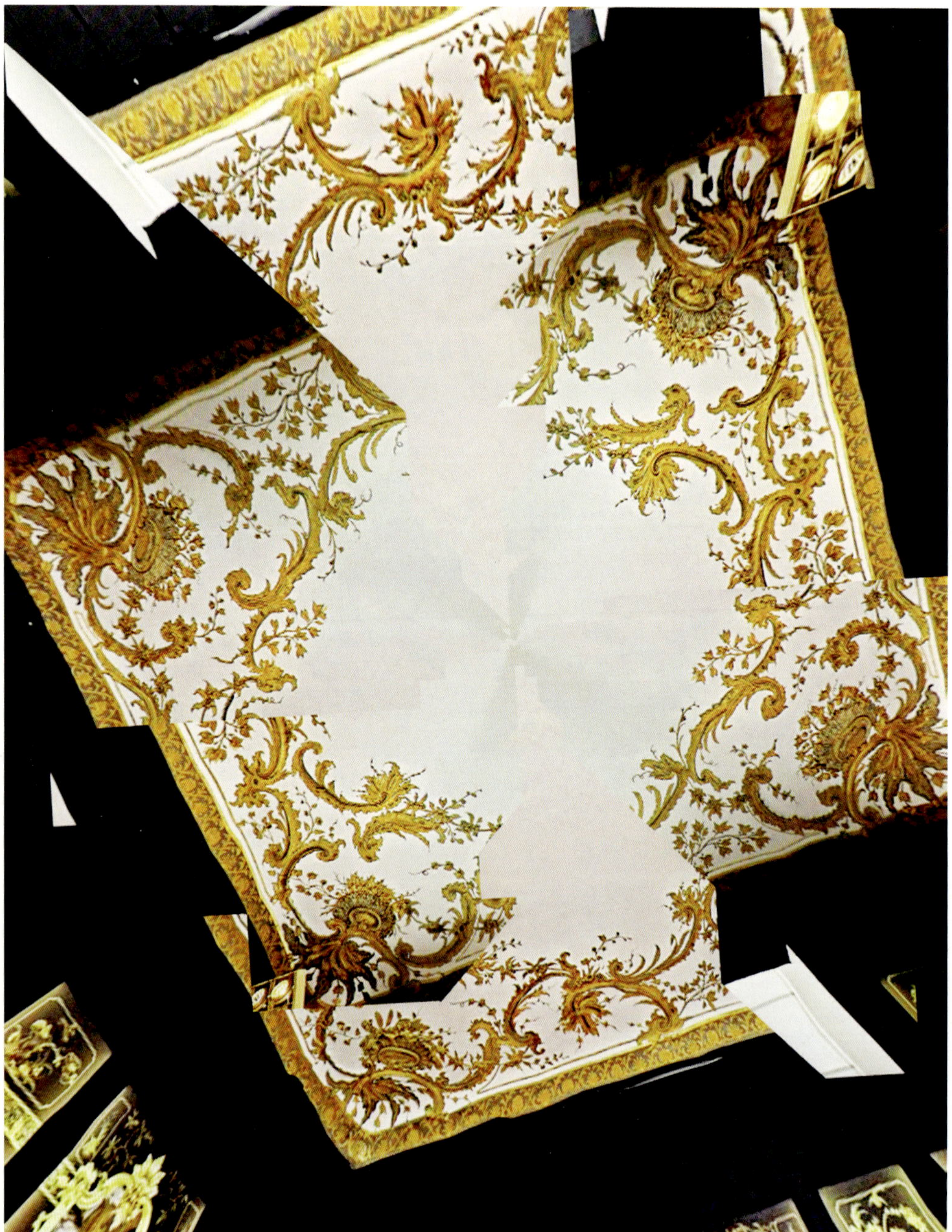

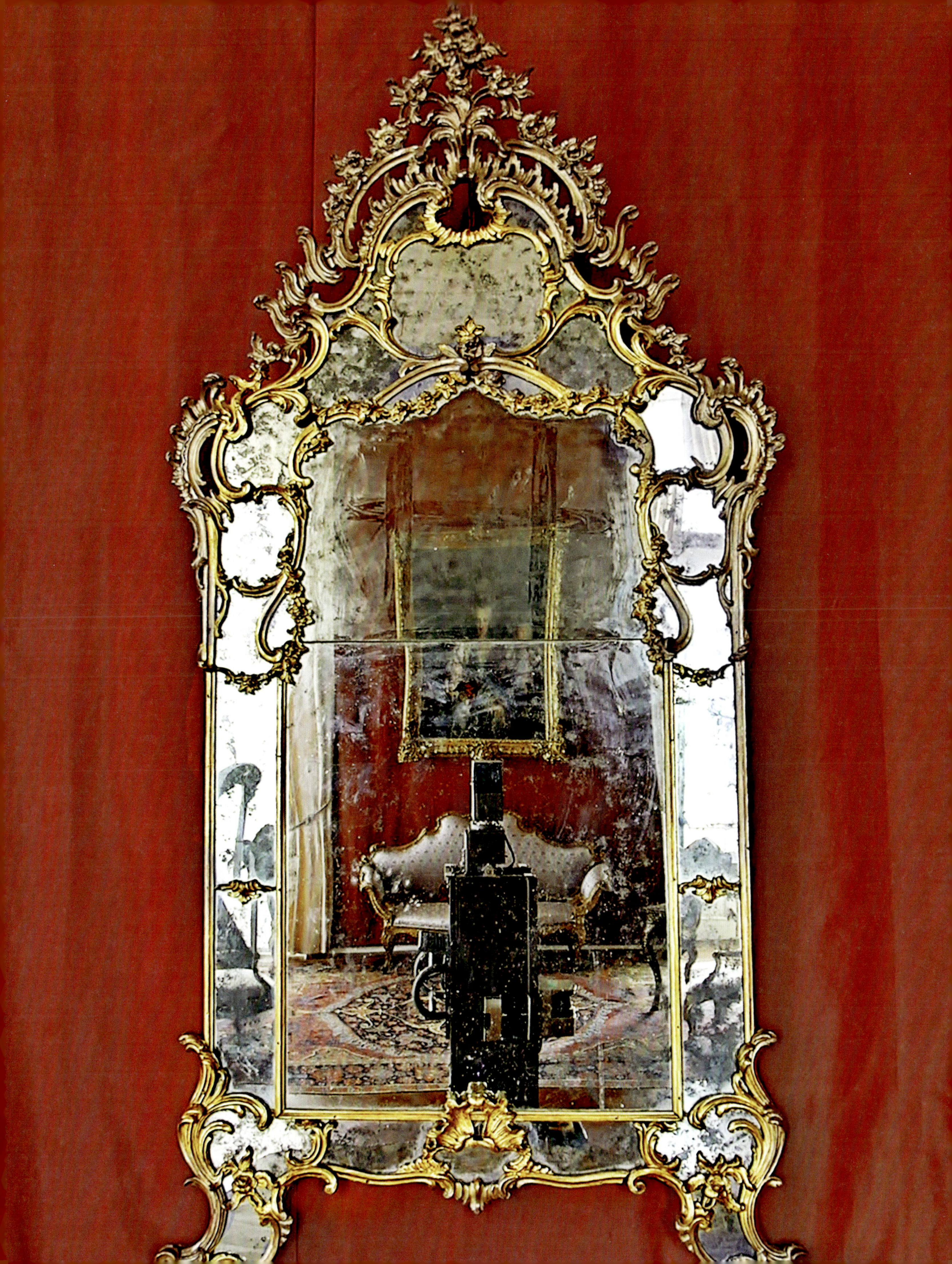

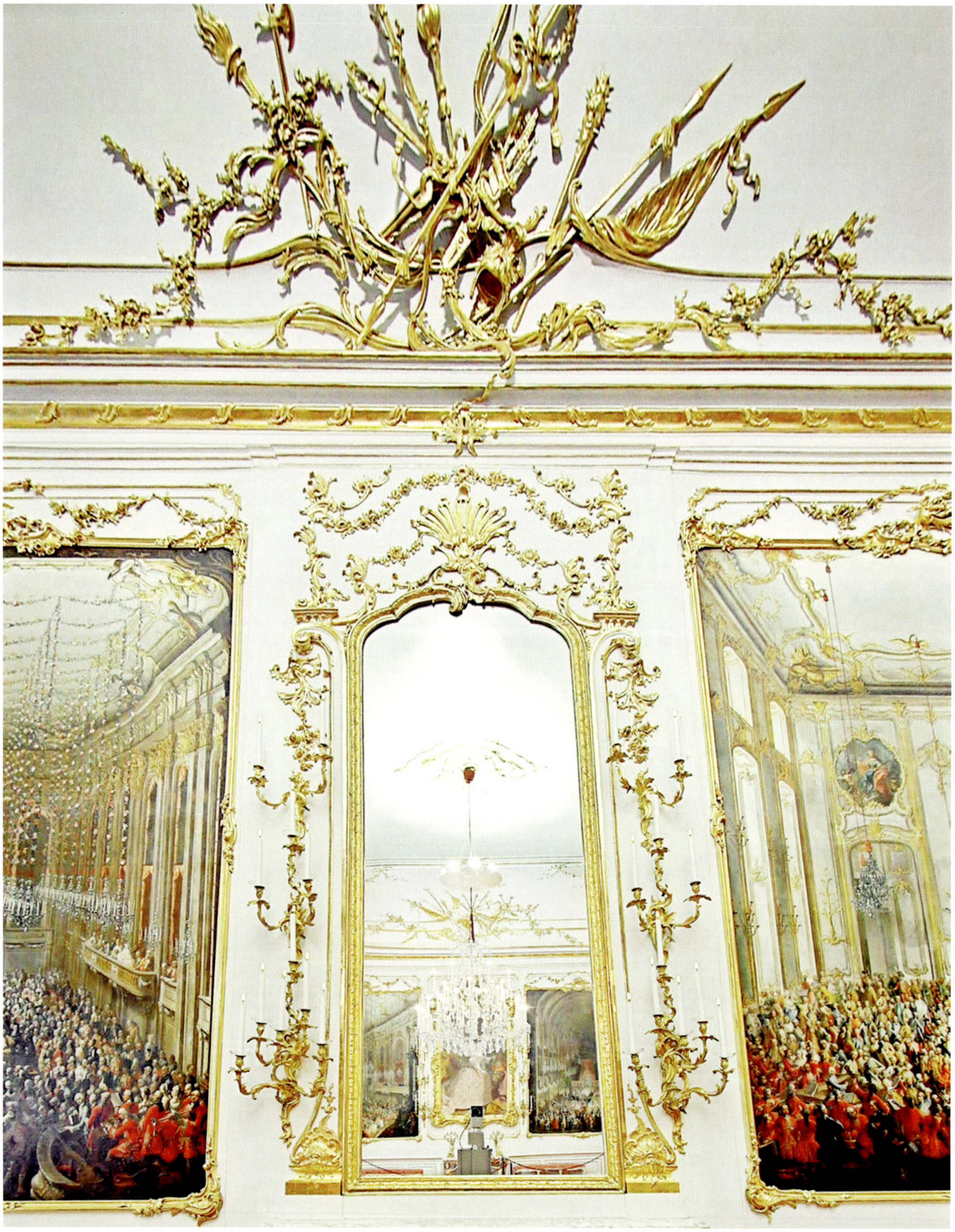

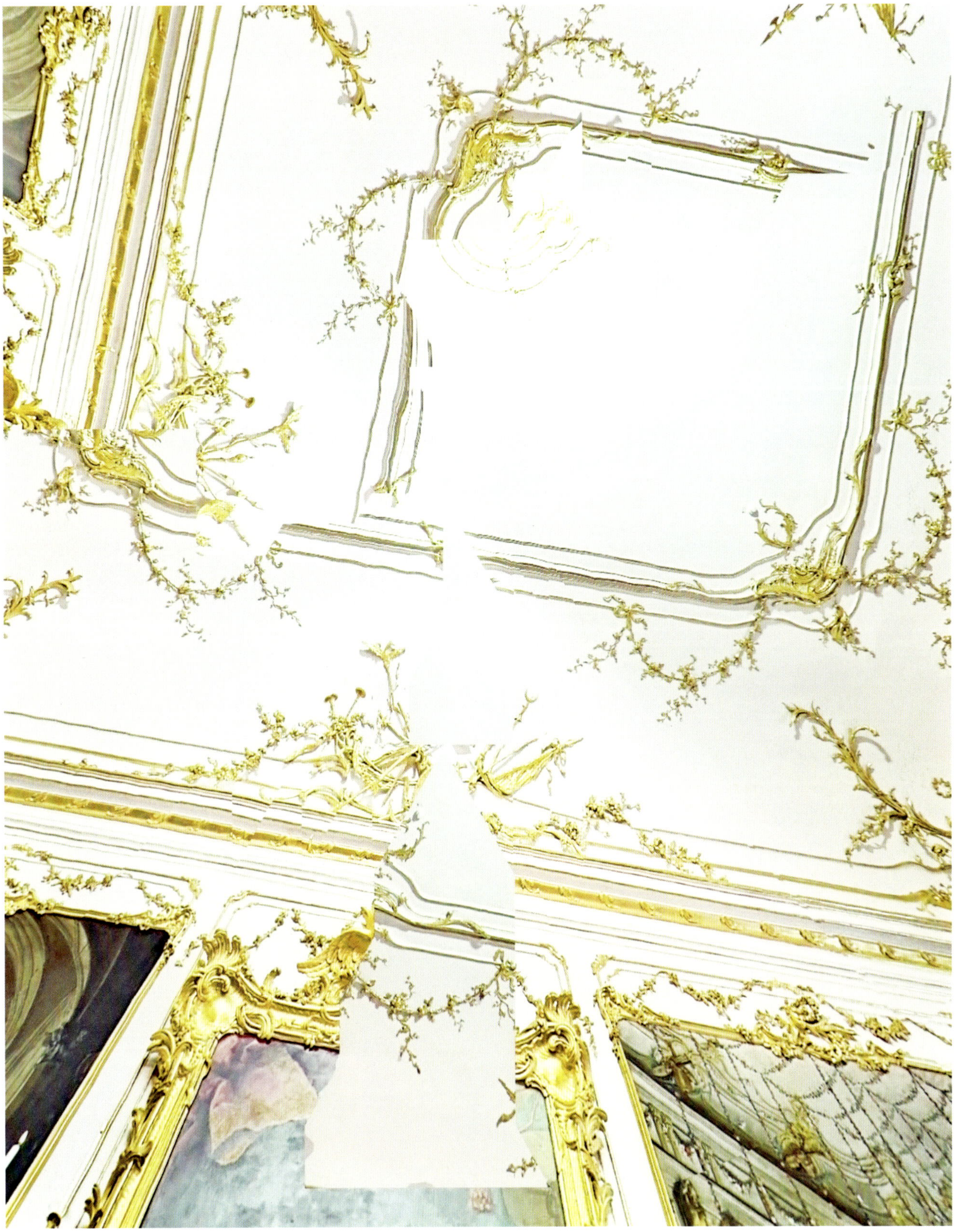

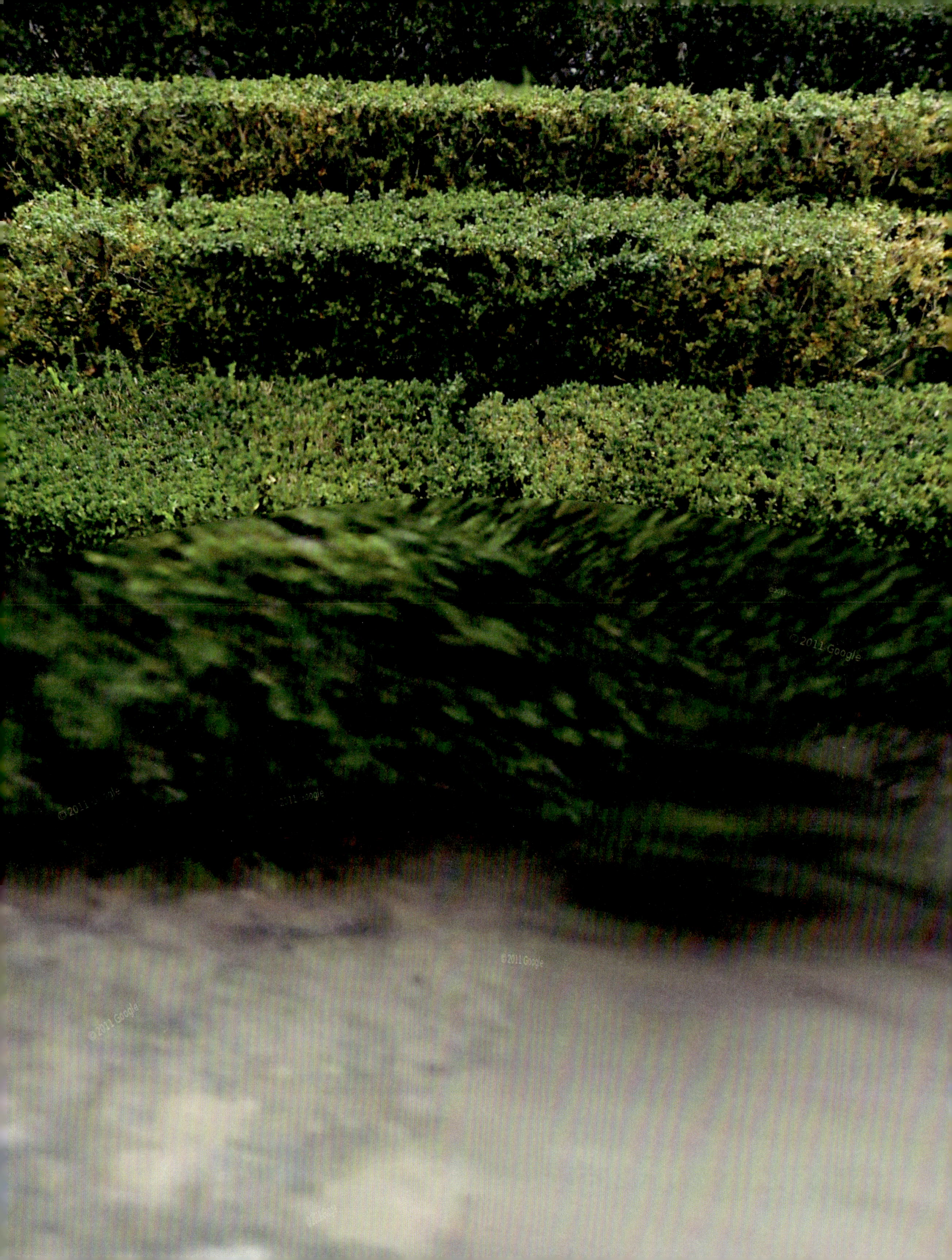
© 2011 Google

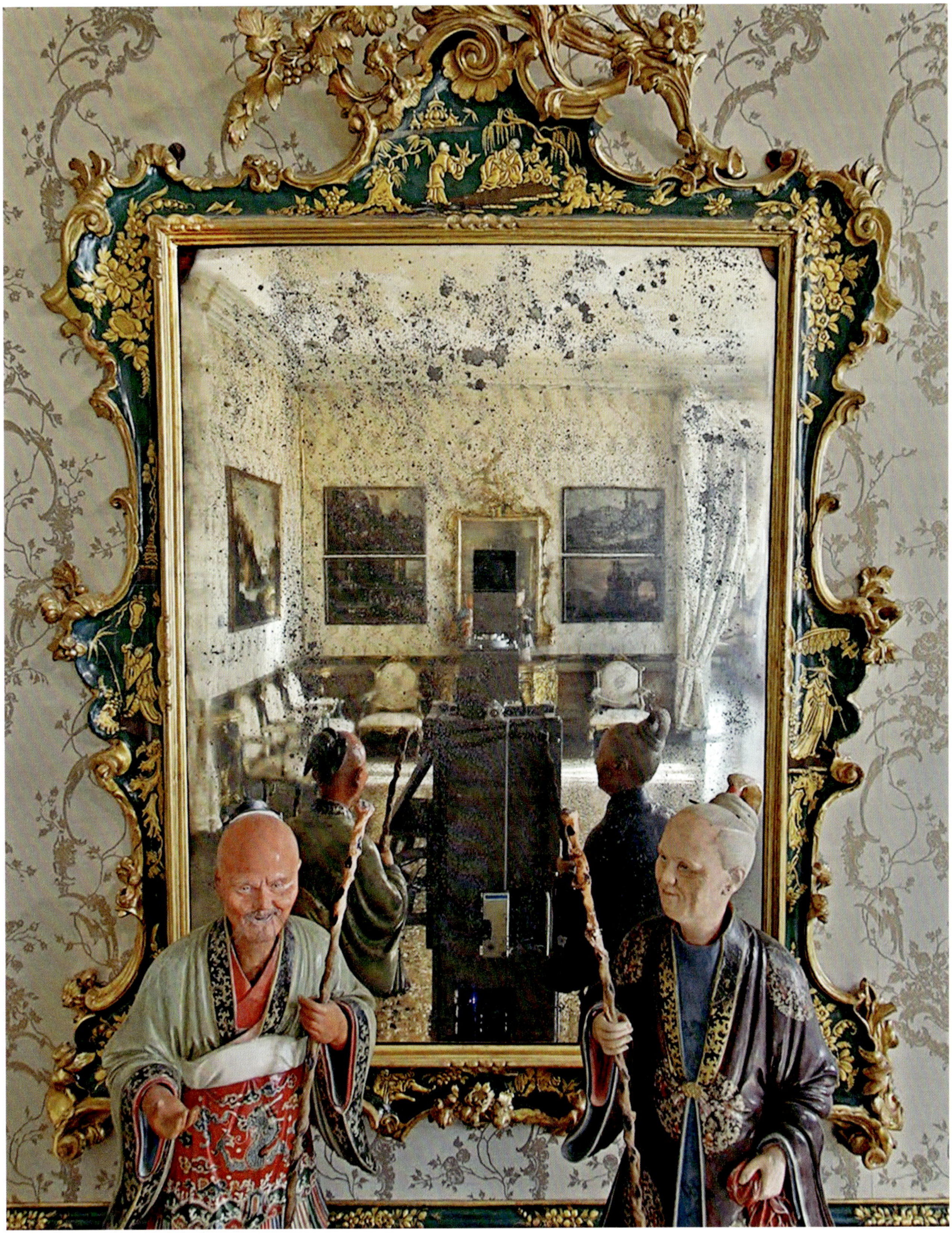

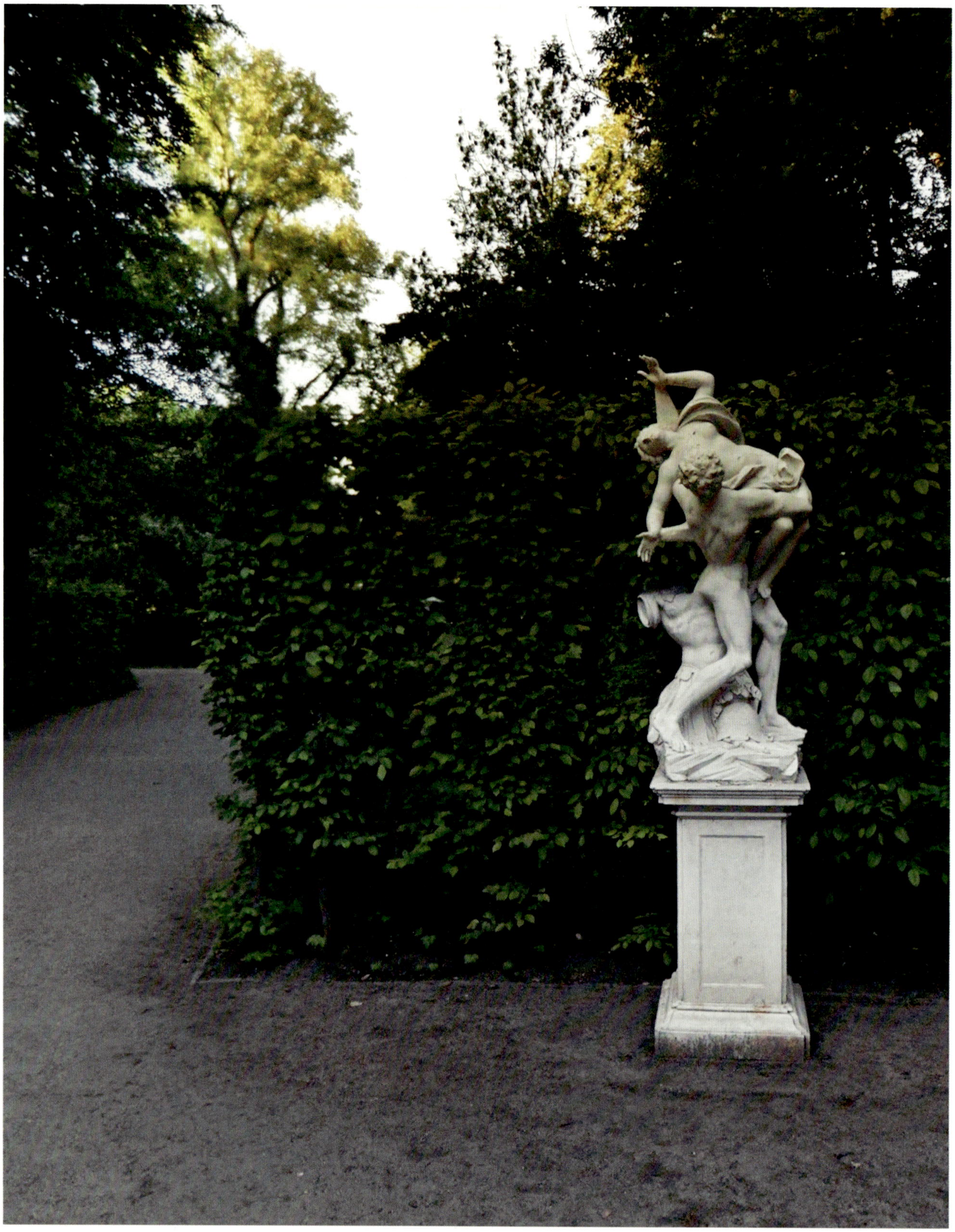

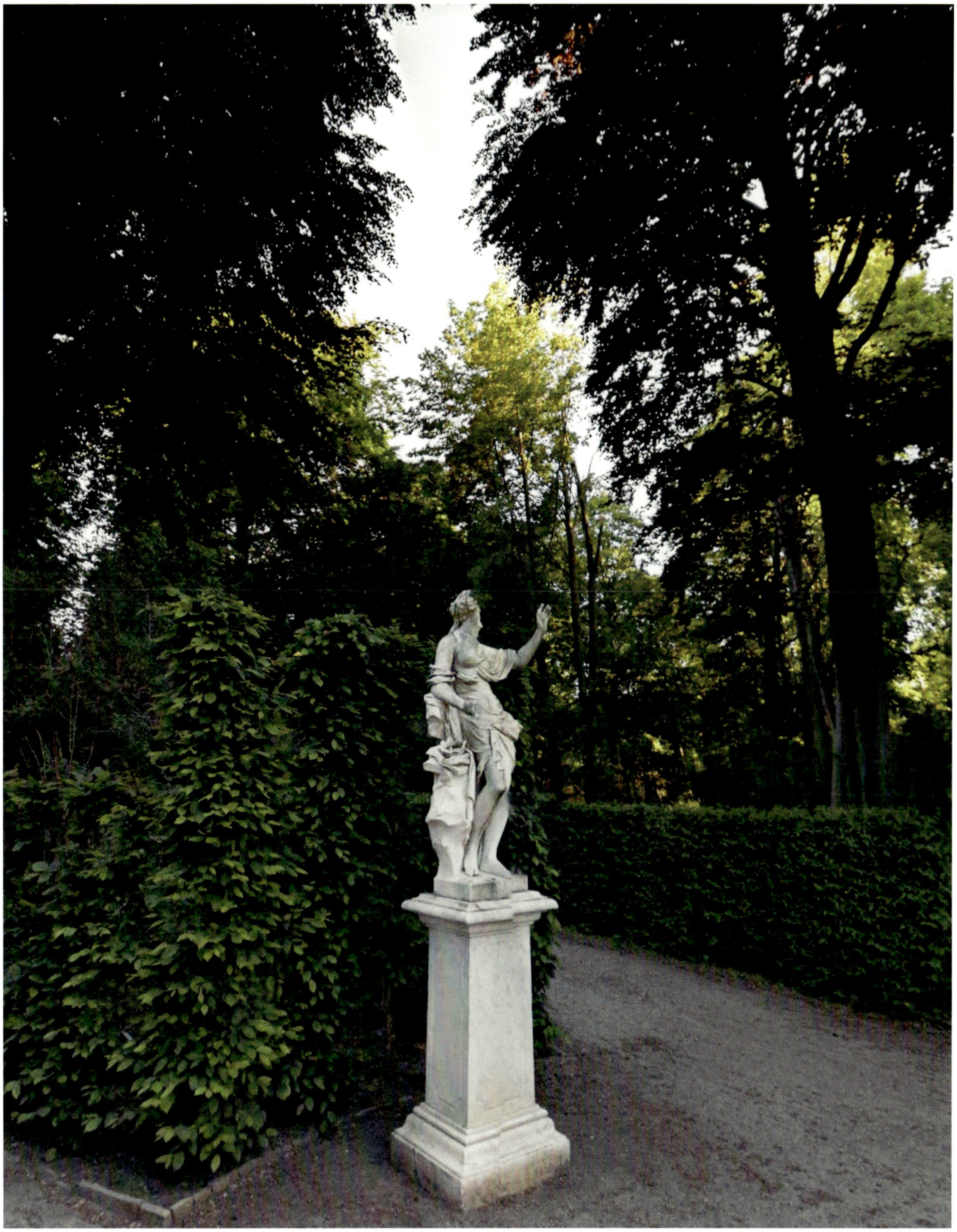

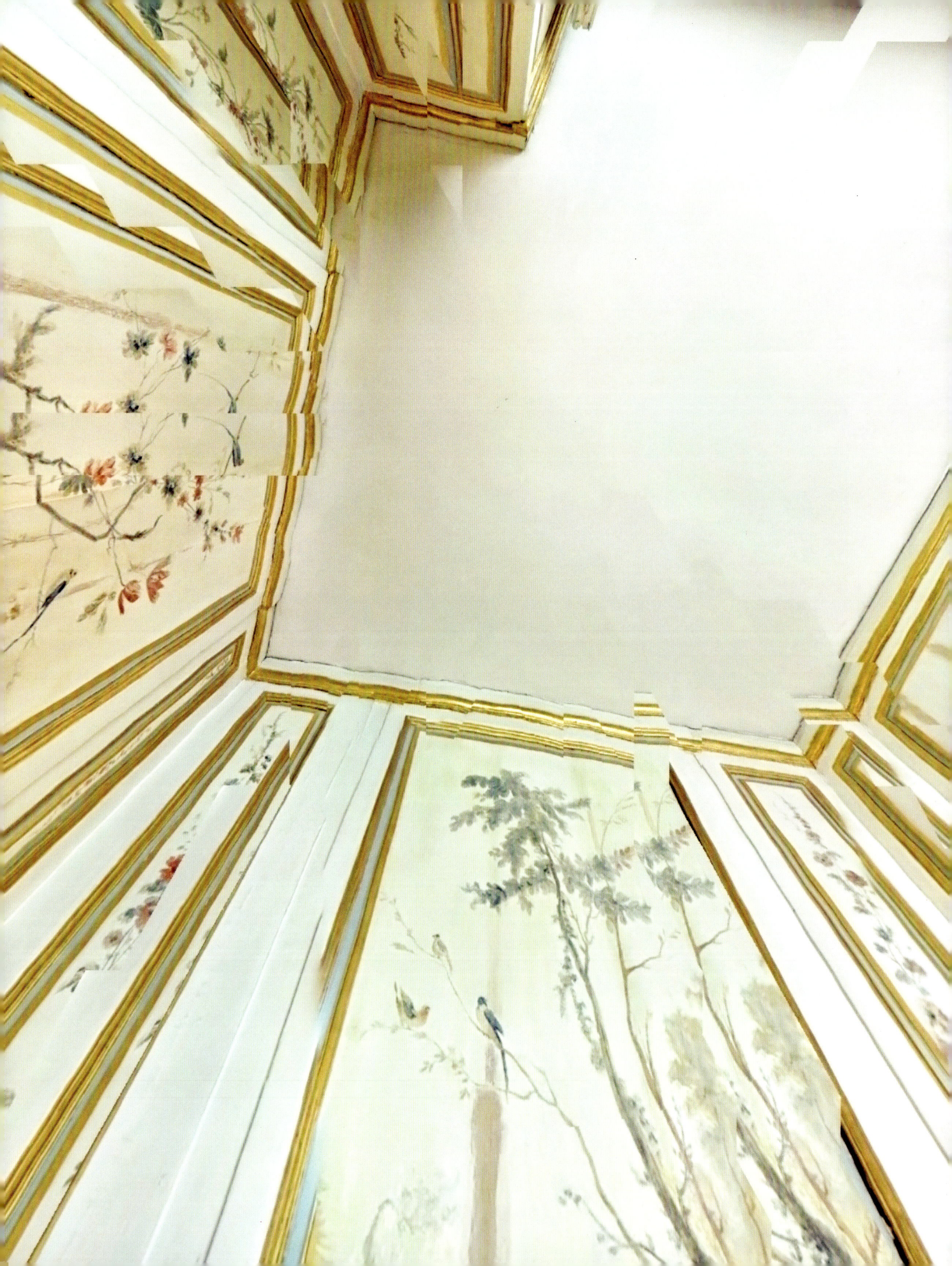

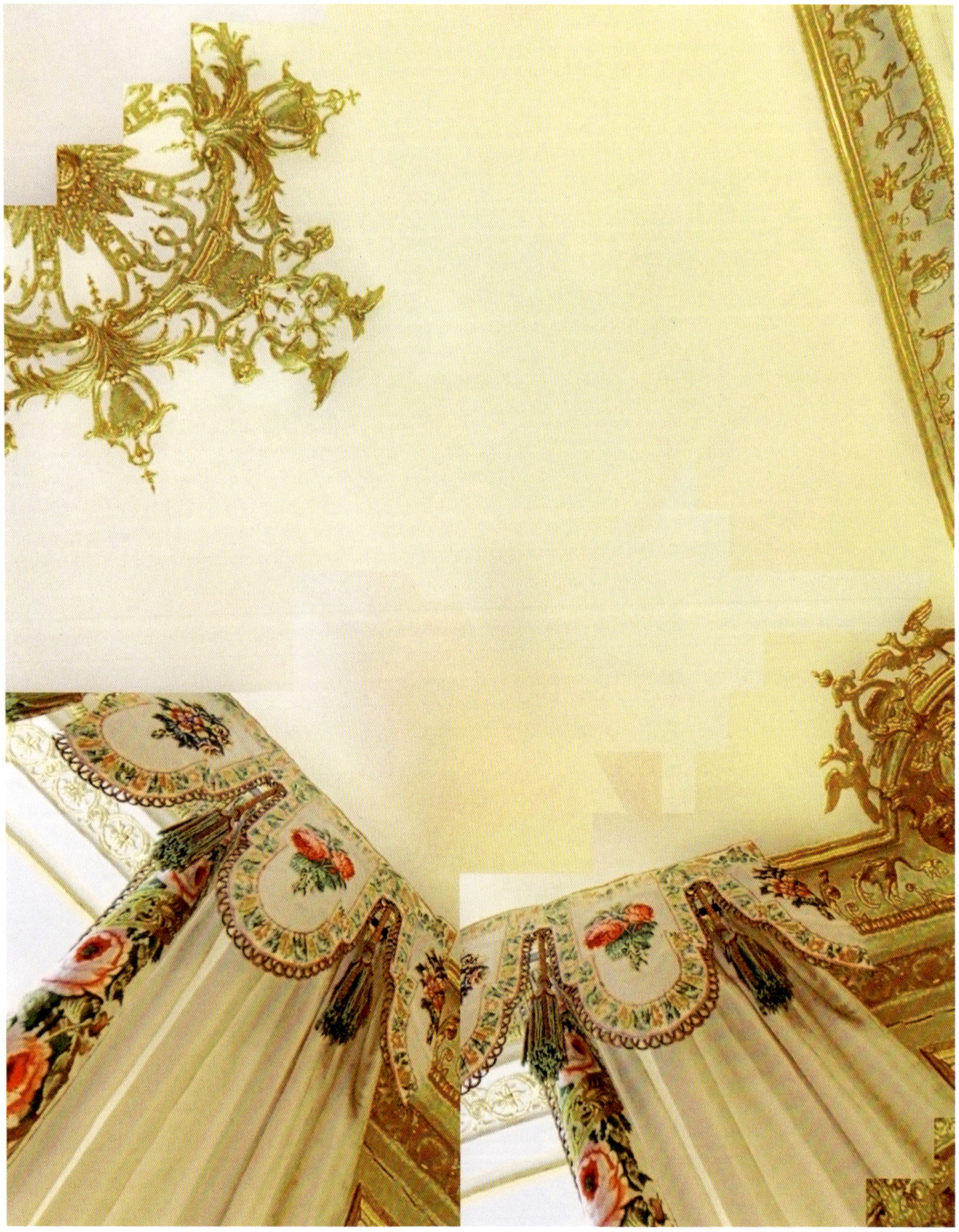

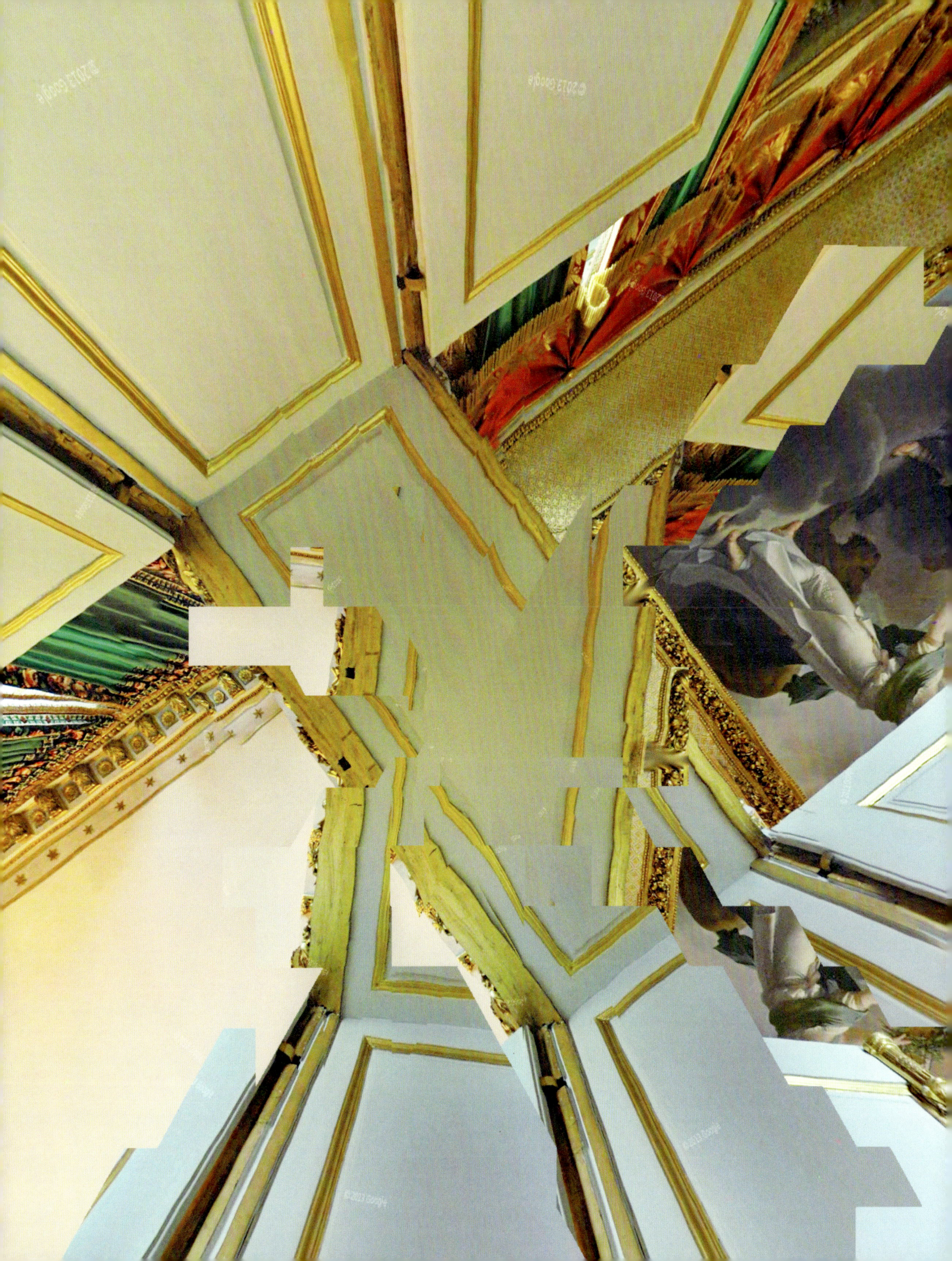

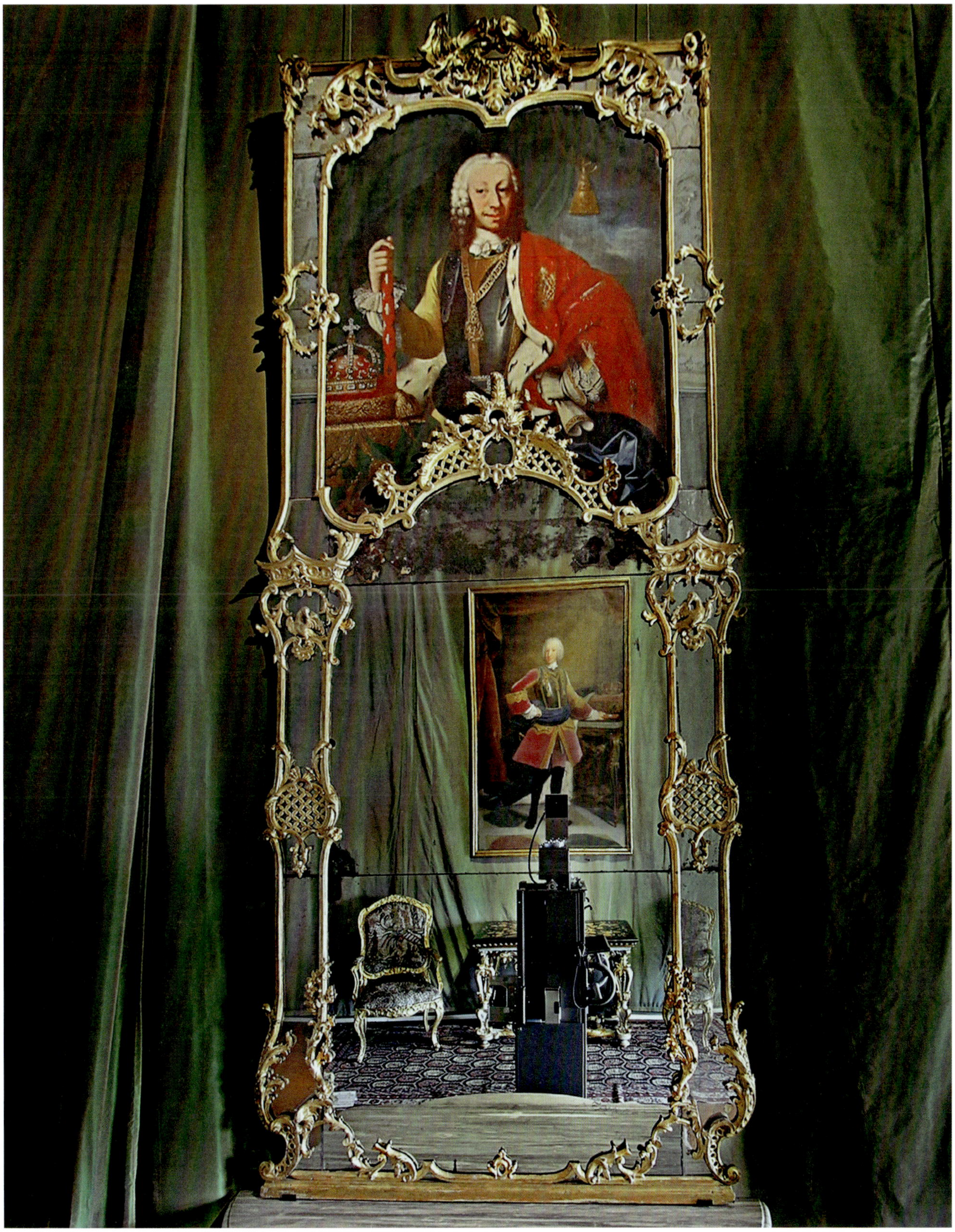

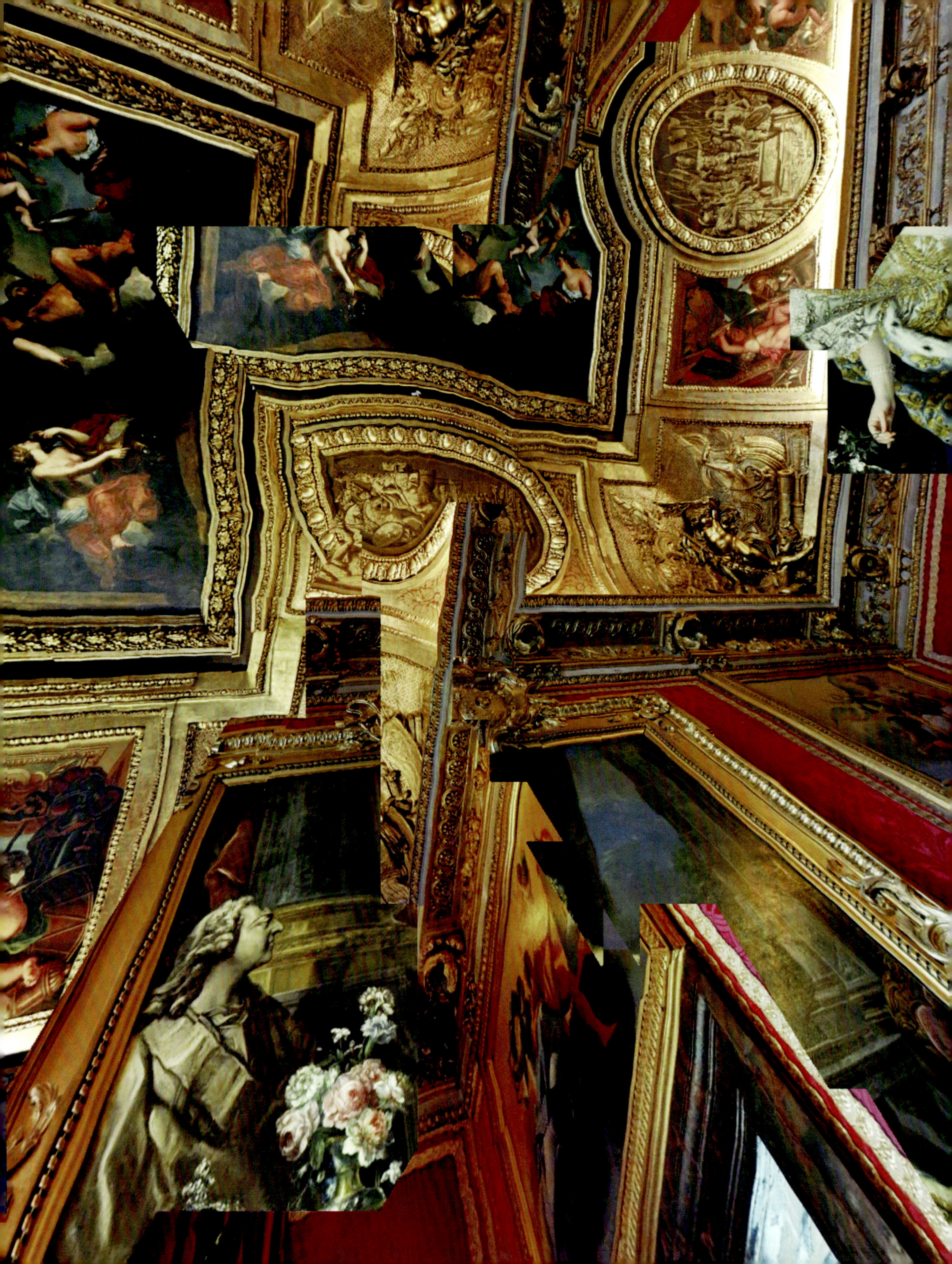

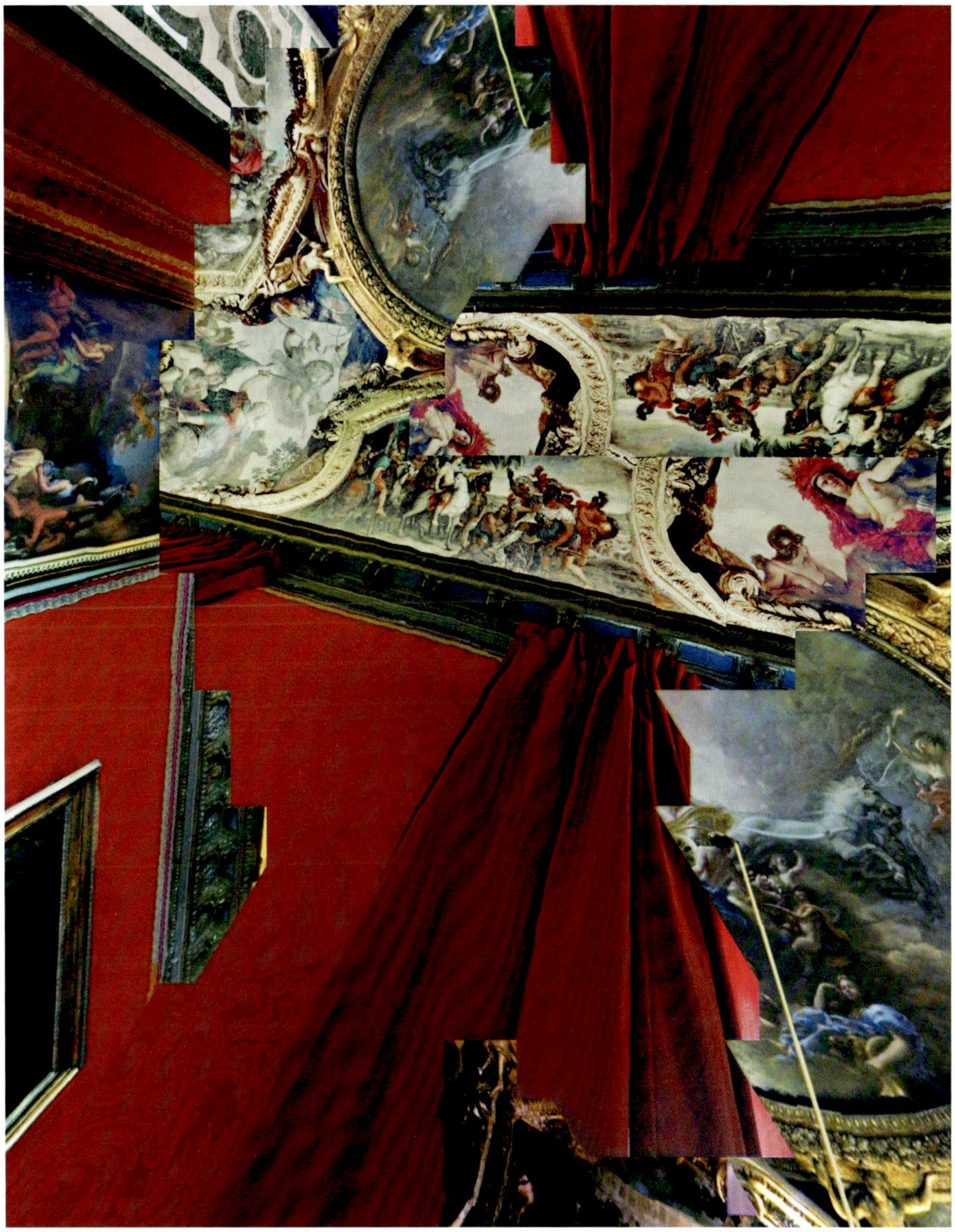

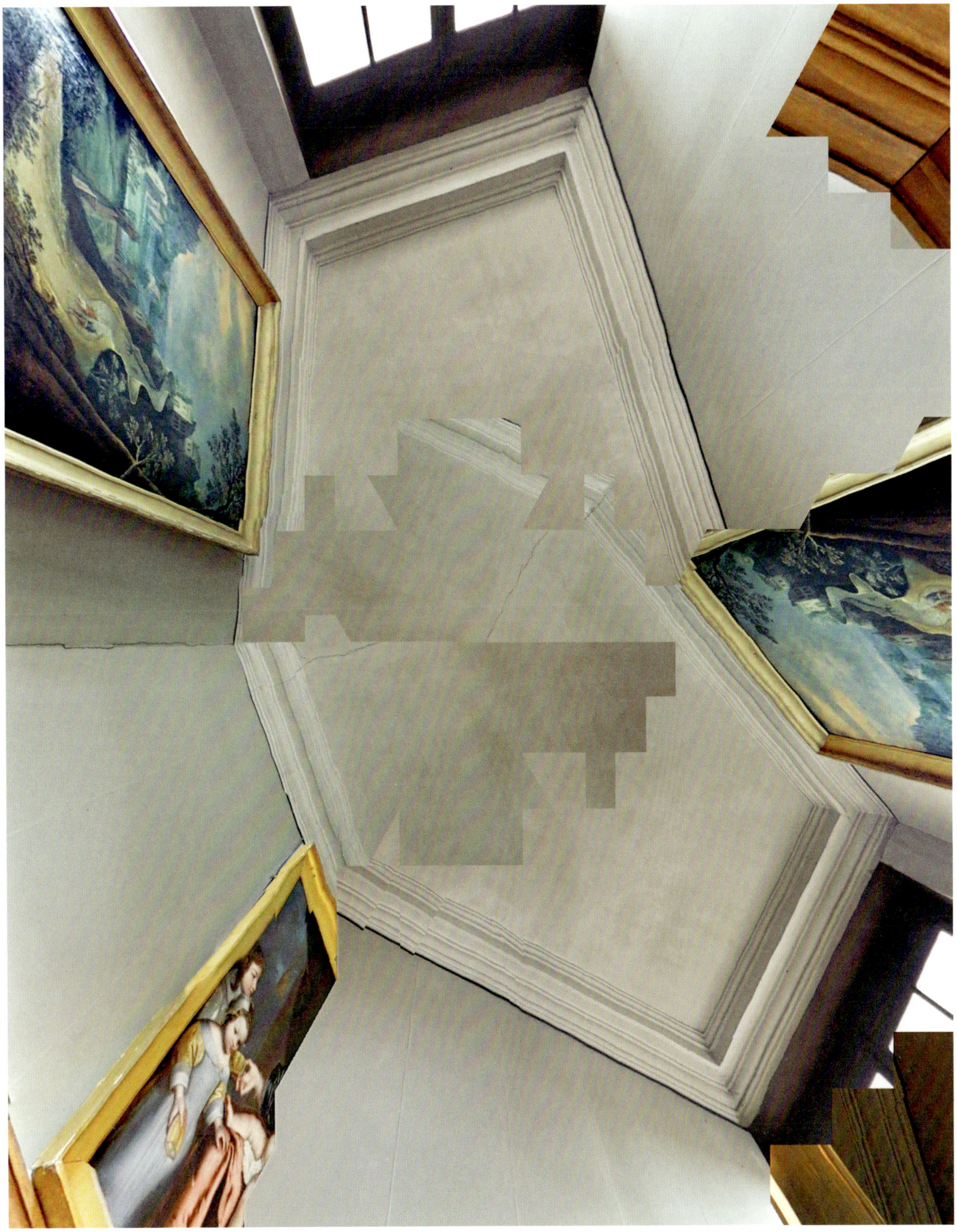

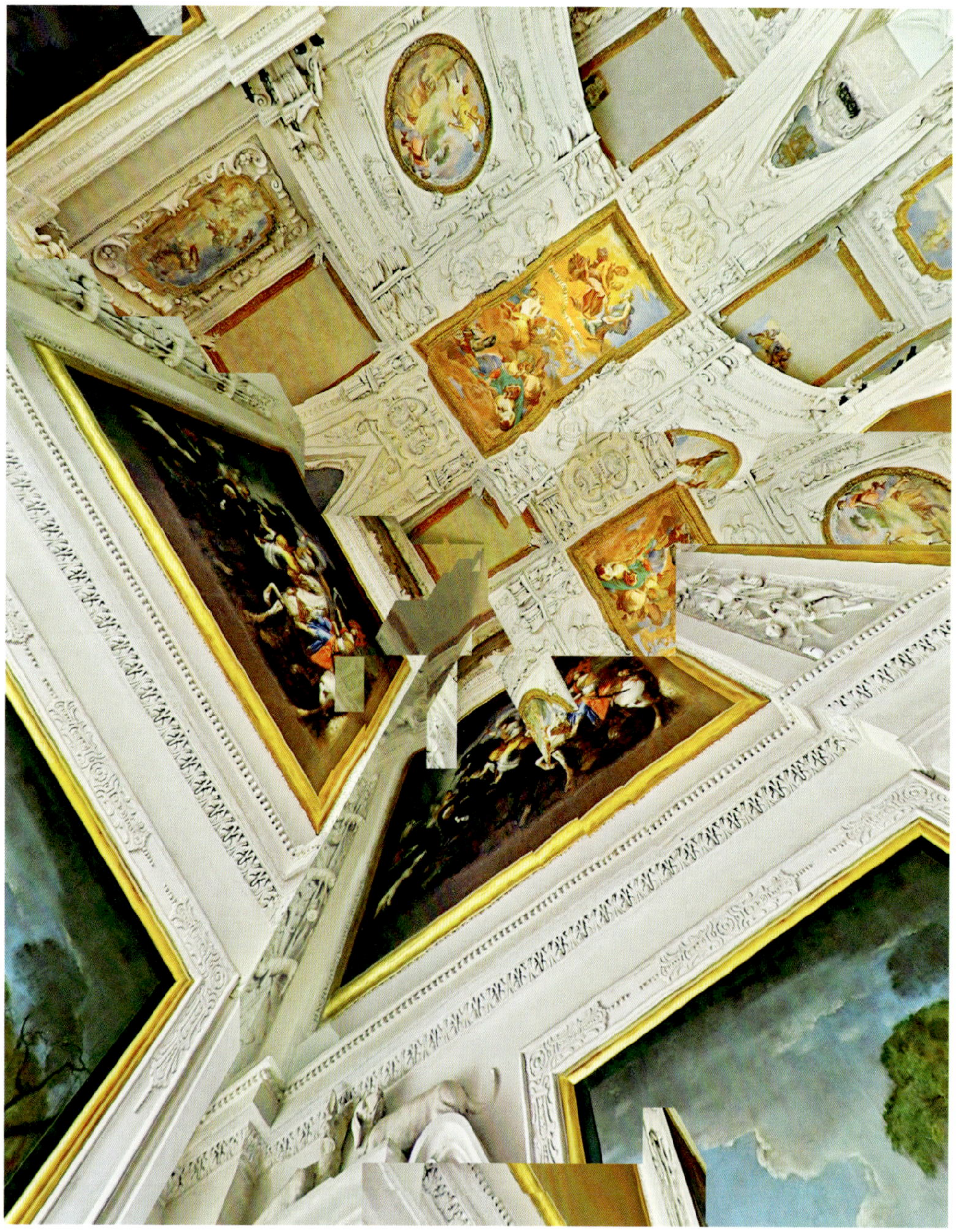

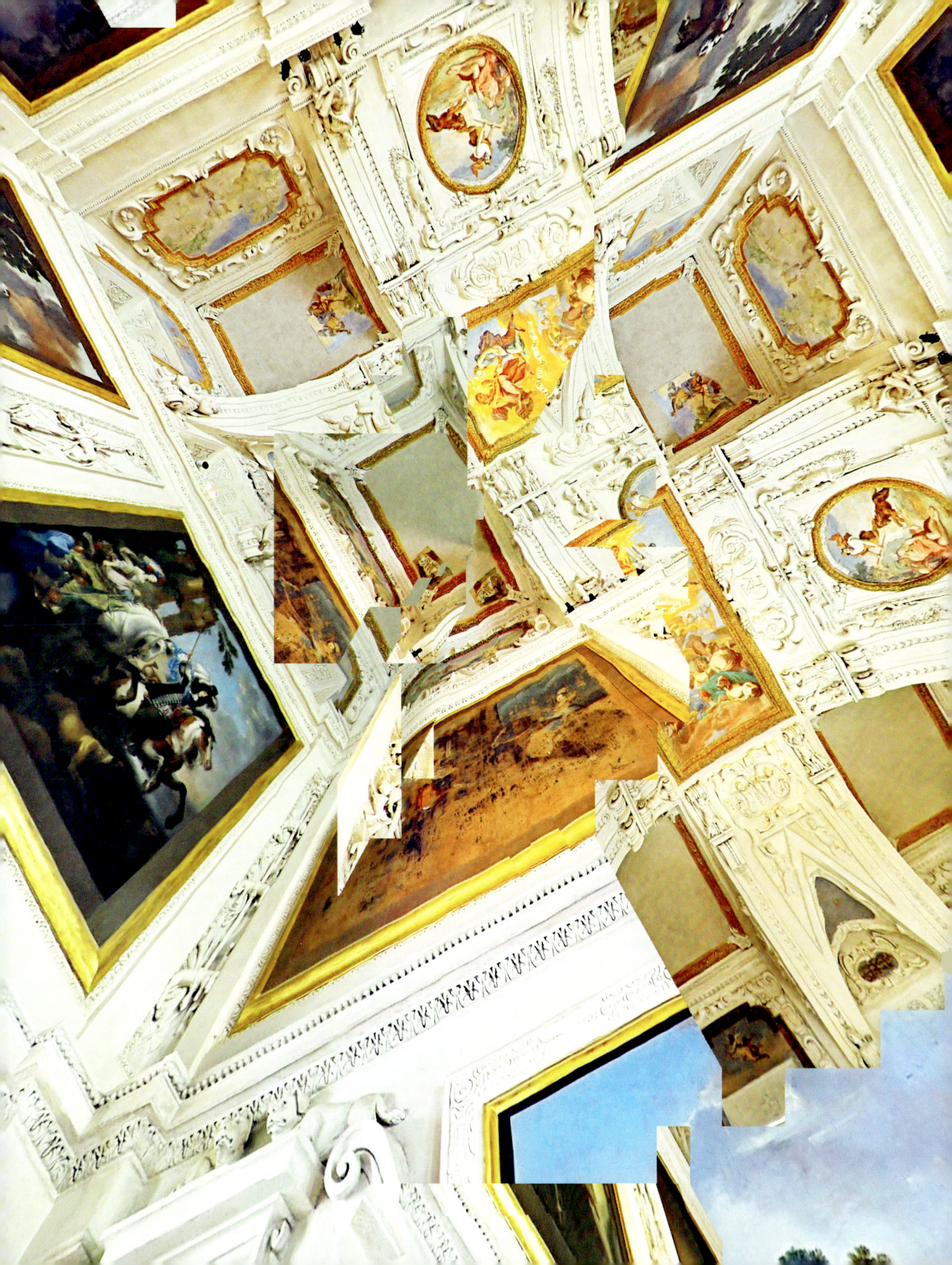

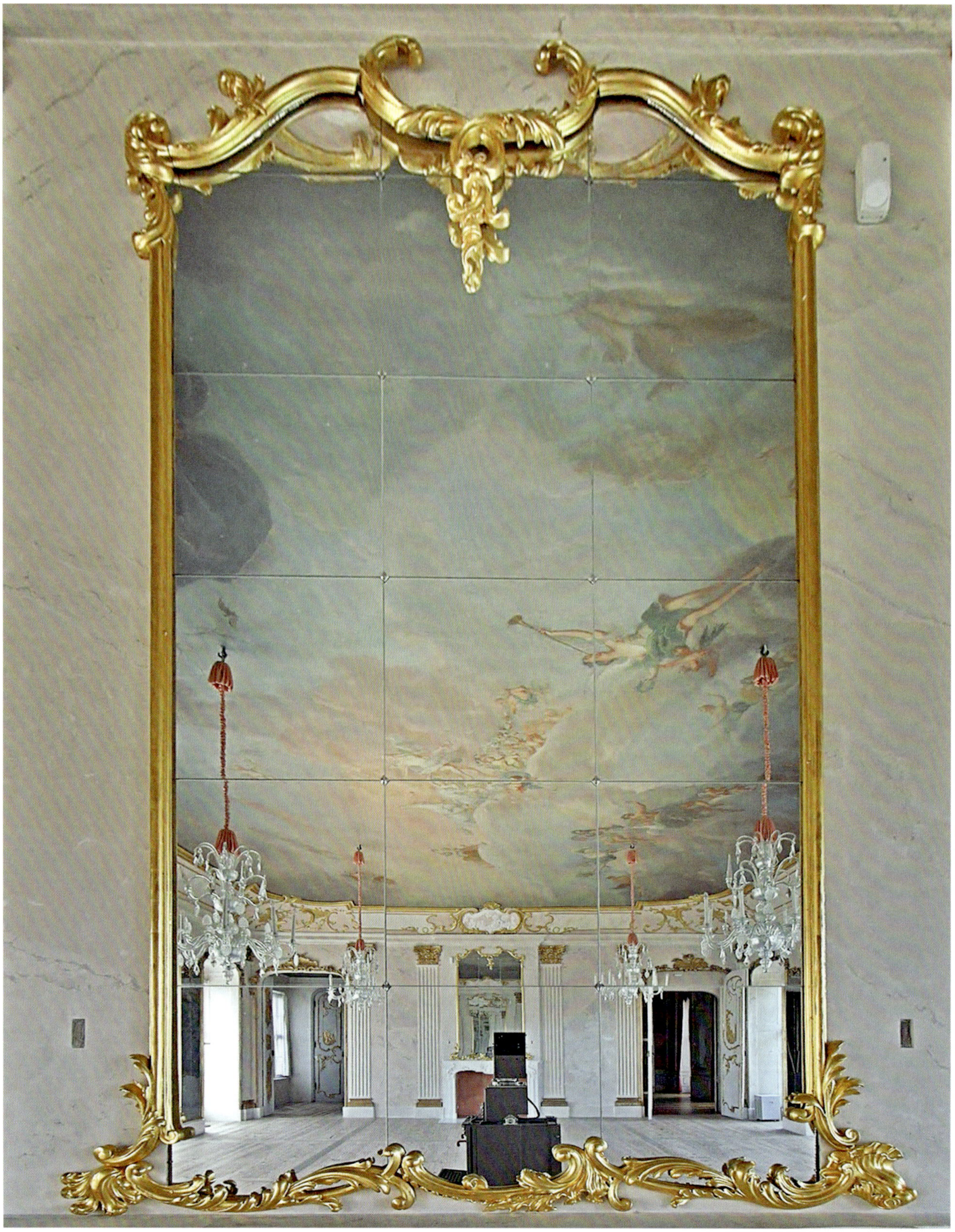

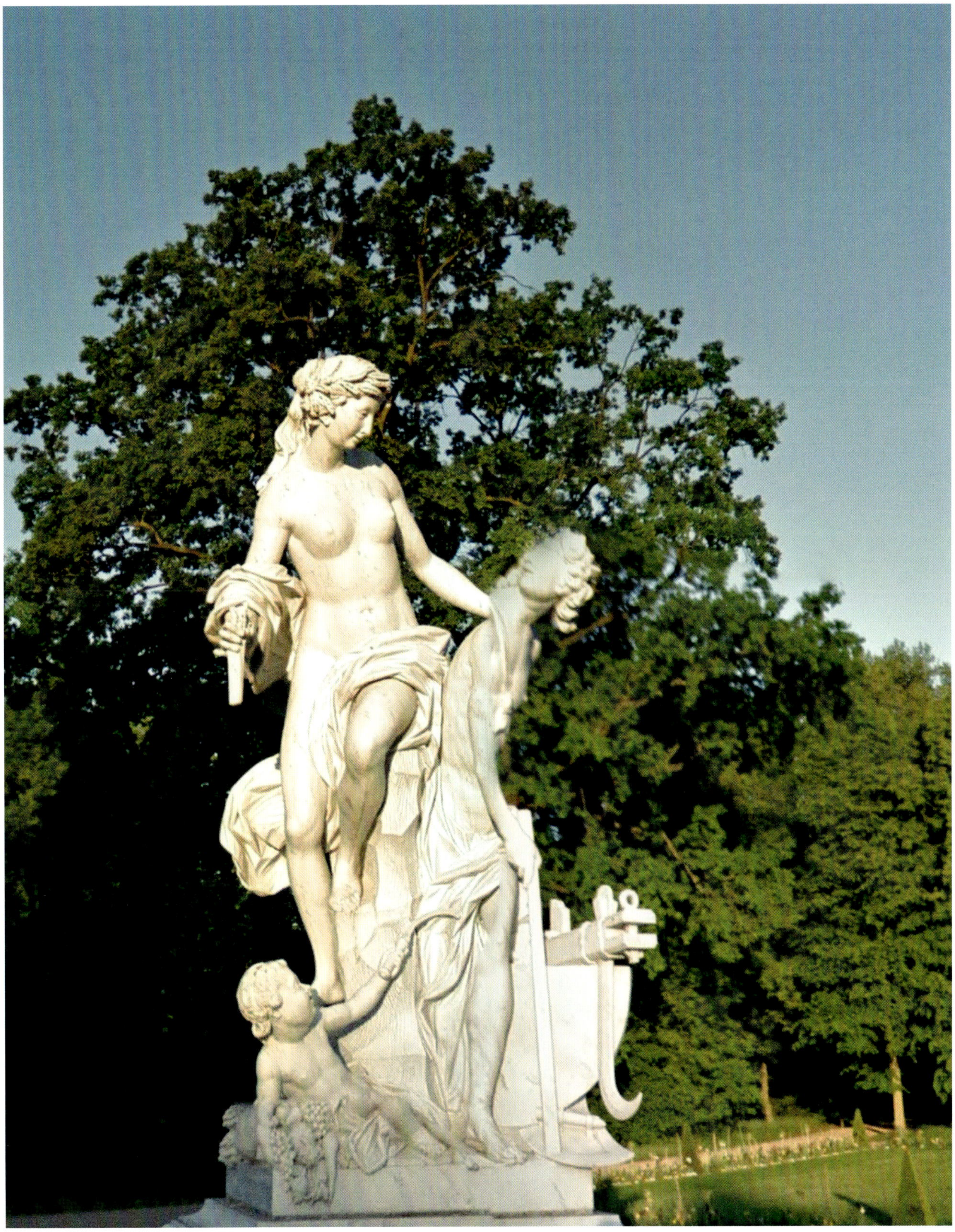

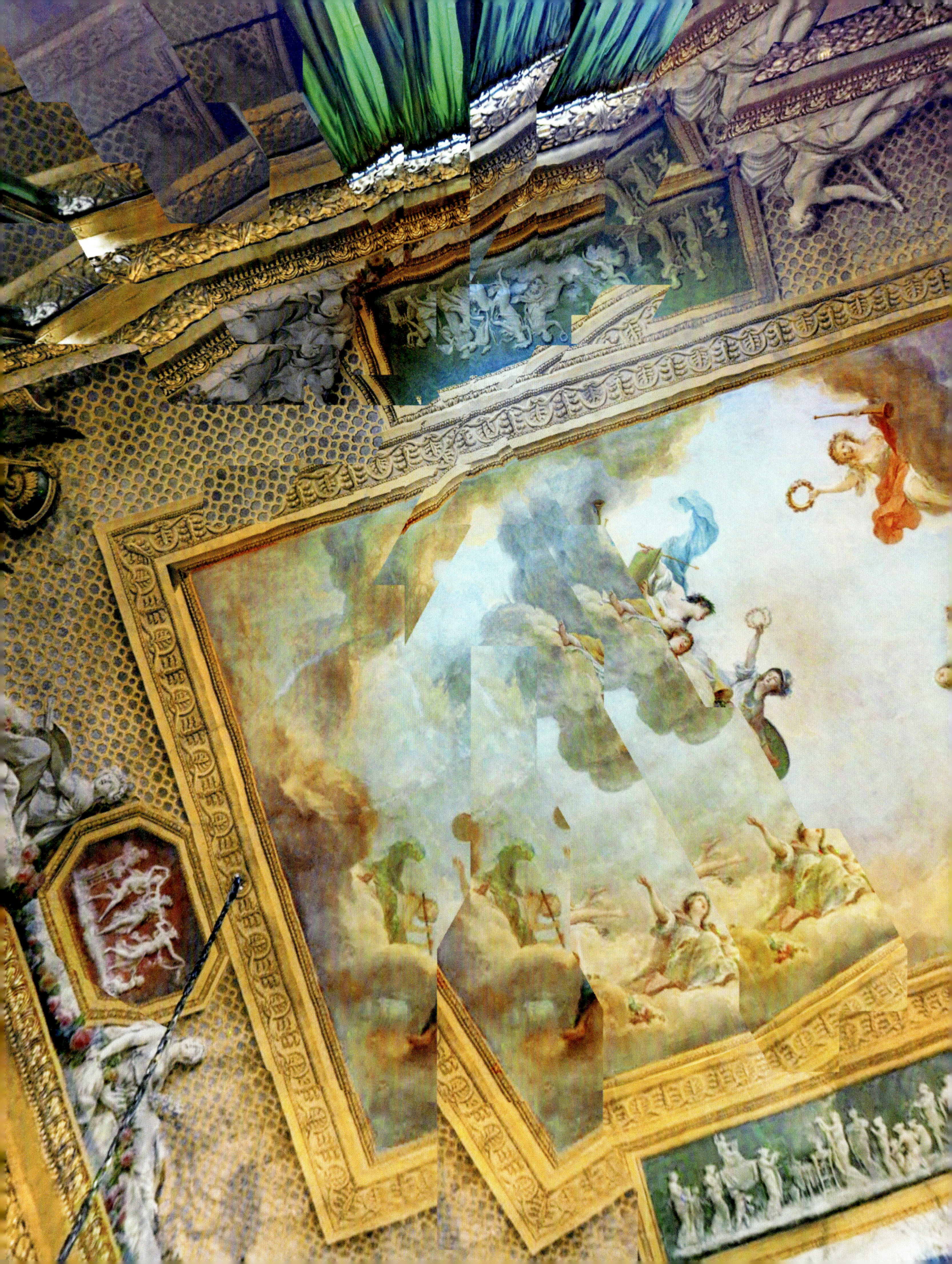

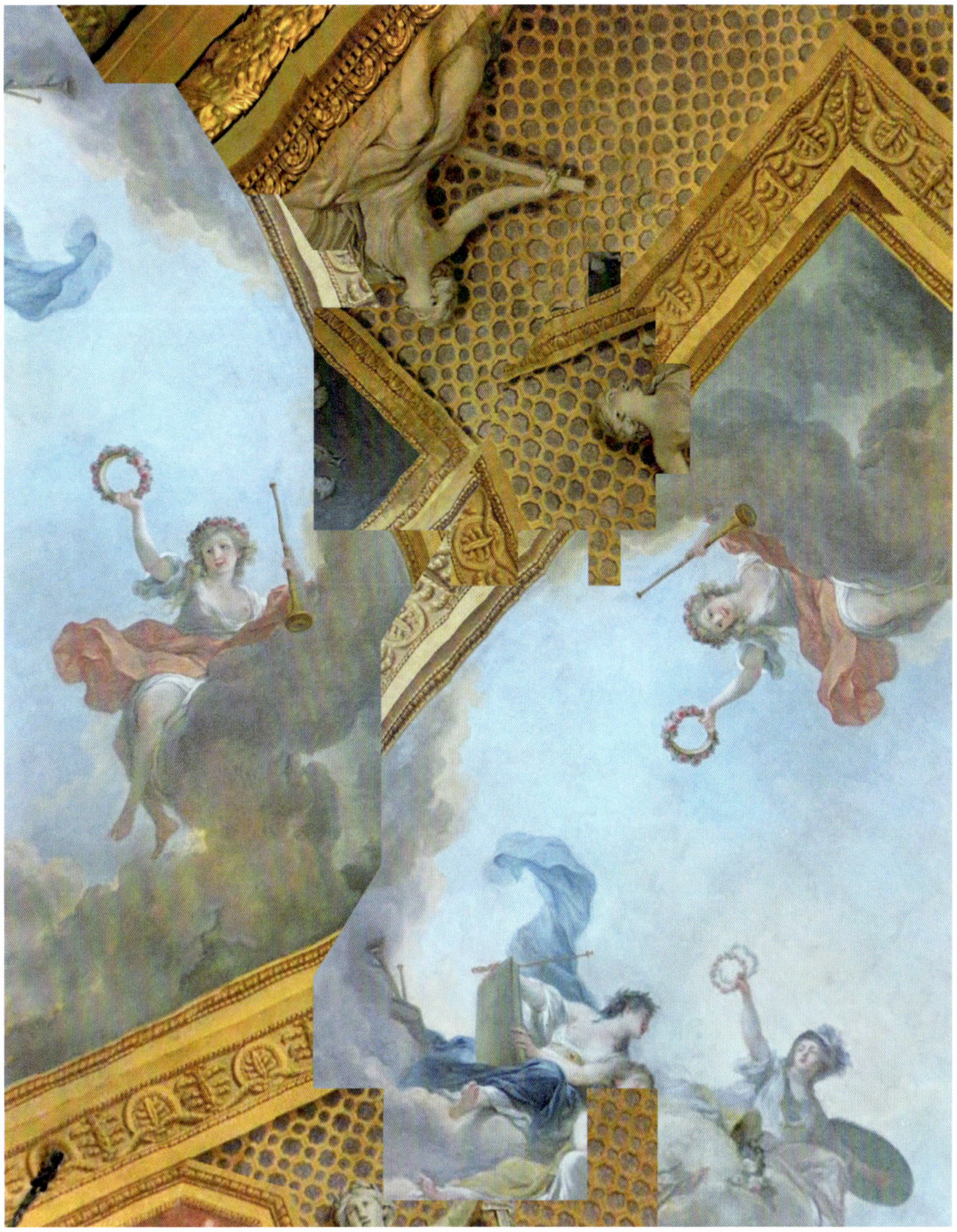

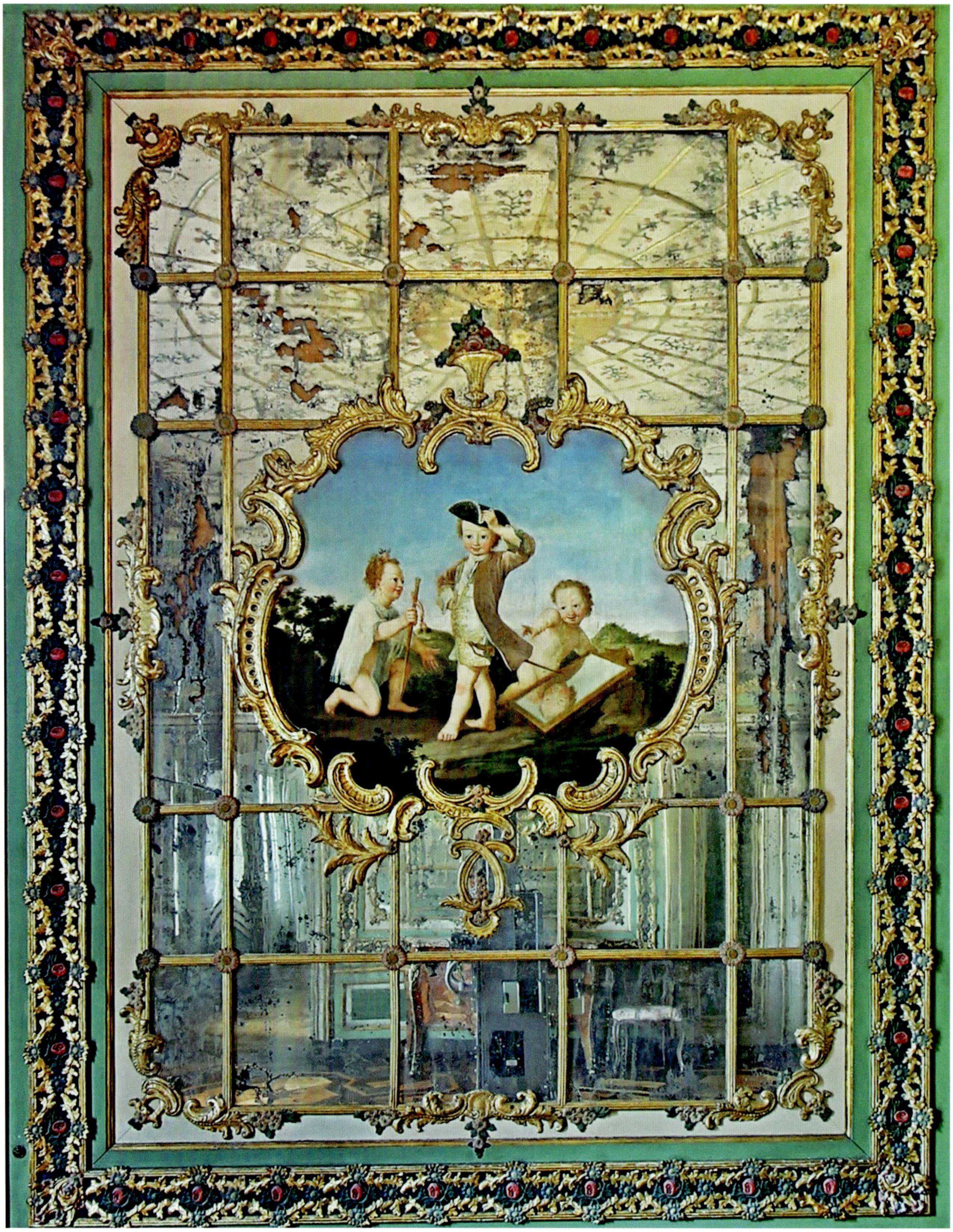

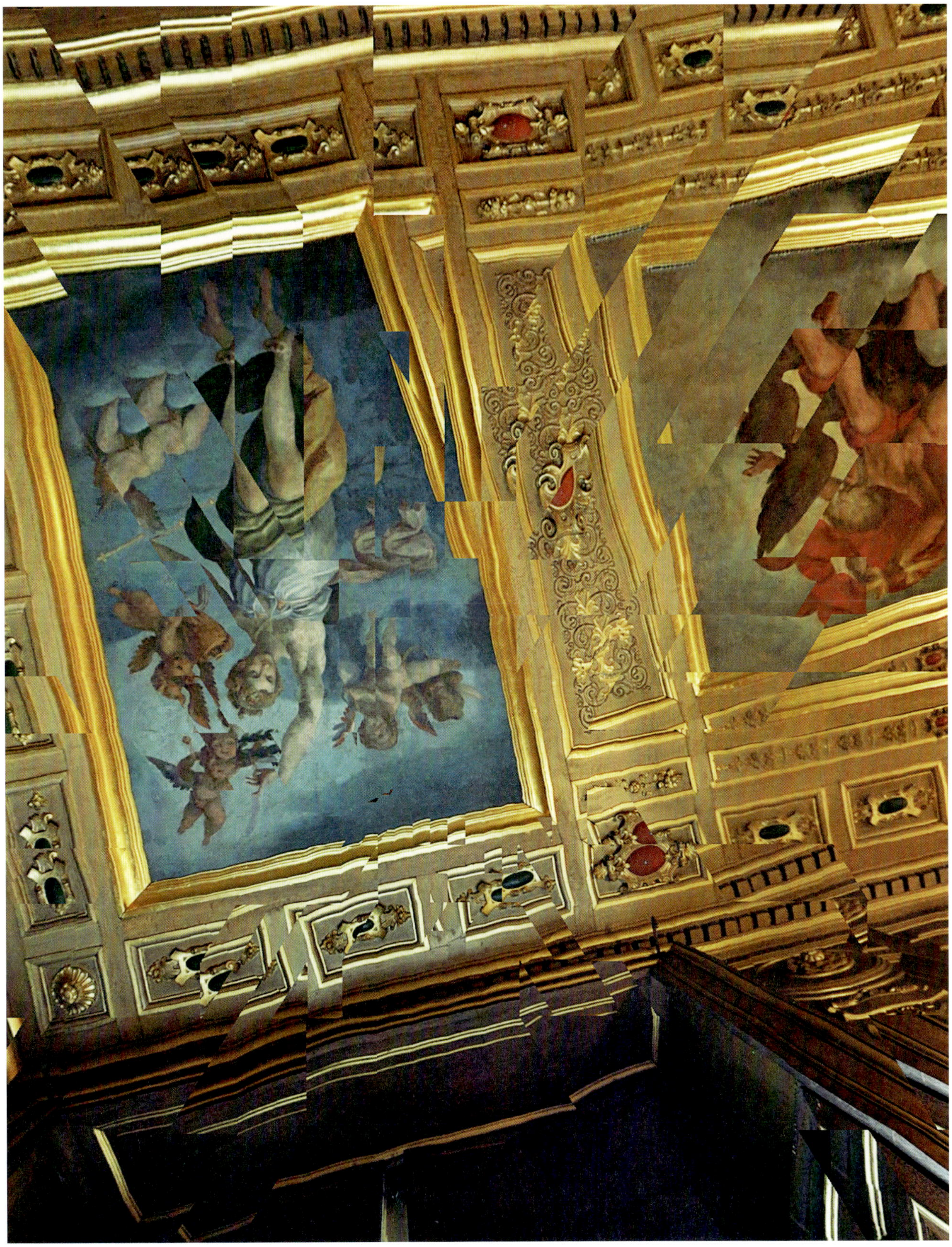

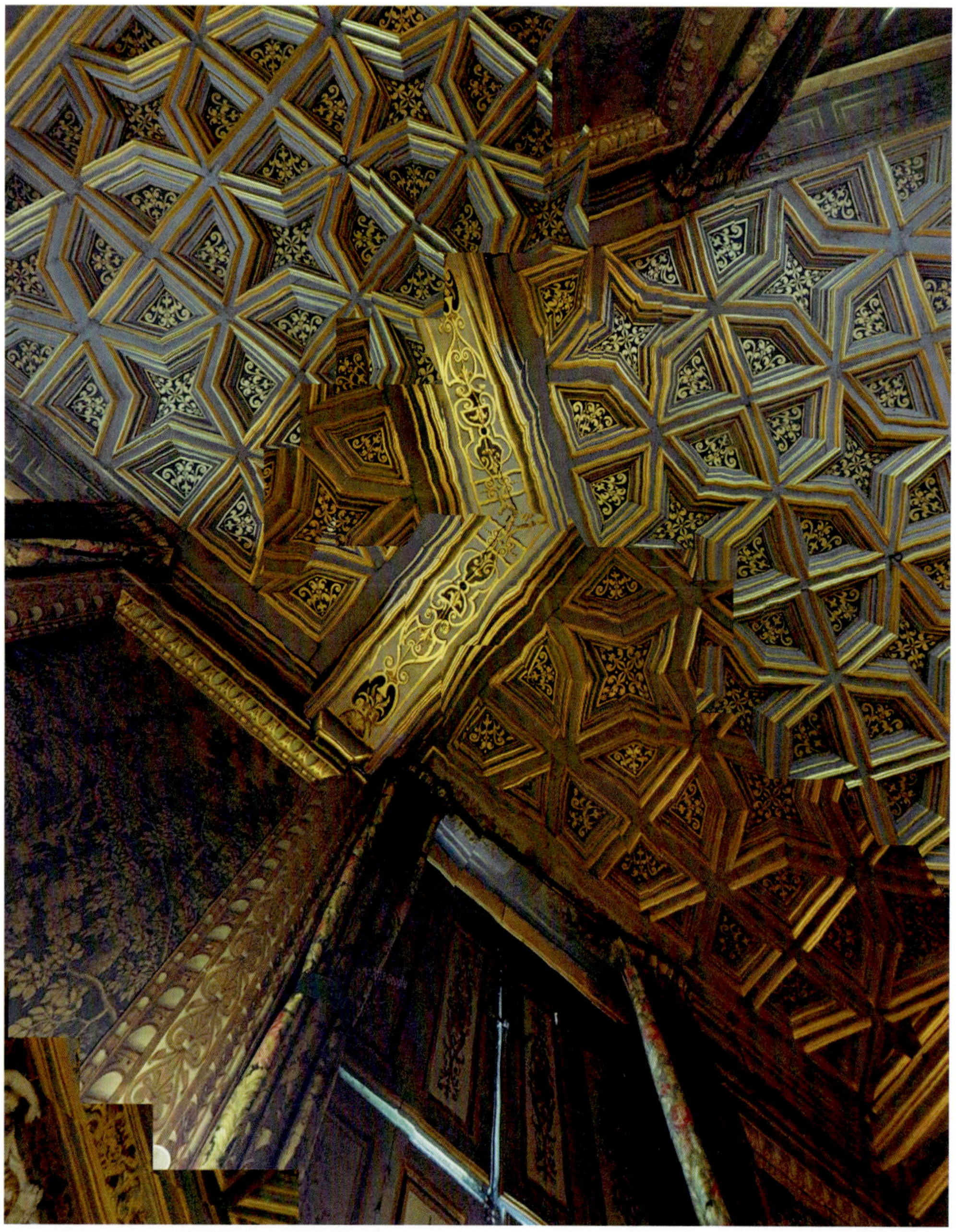

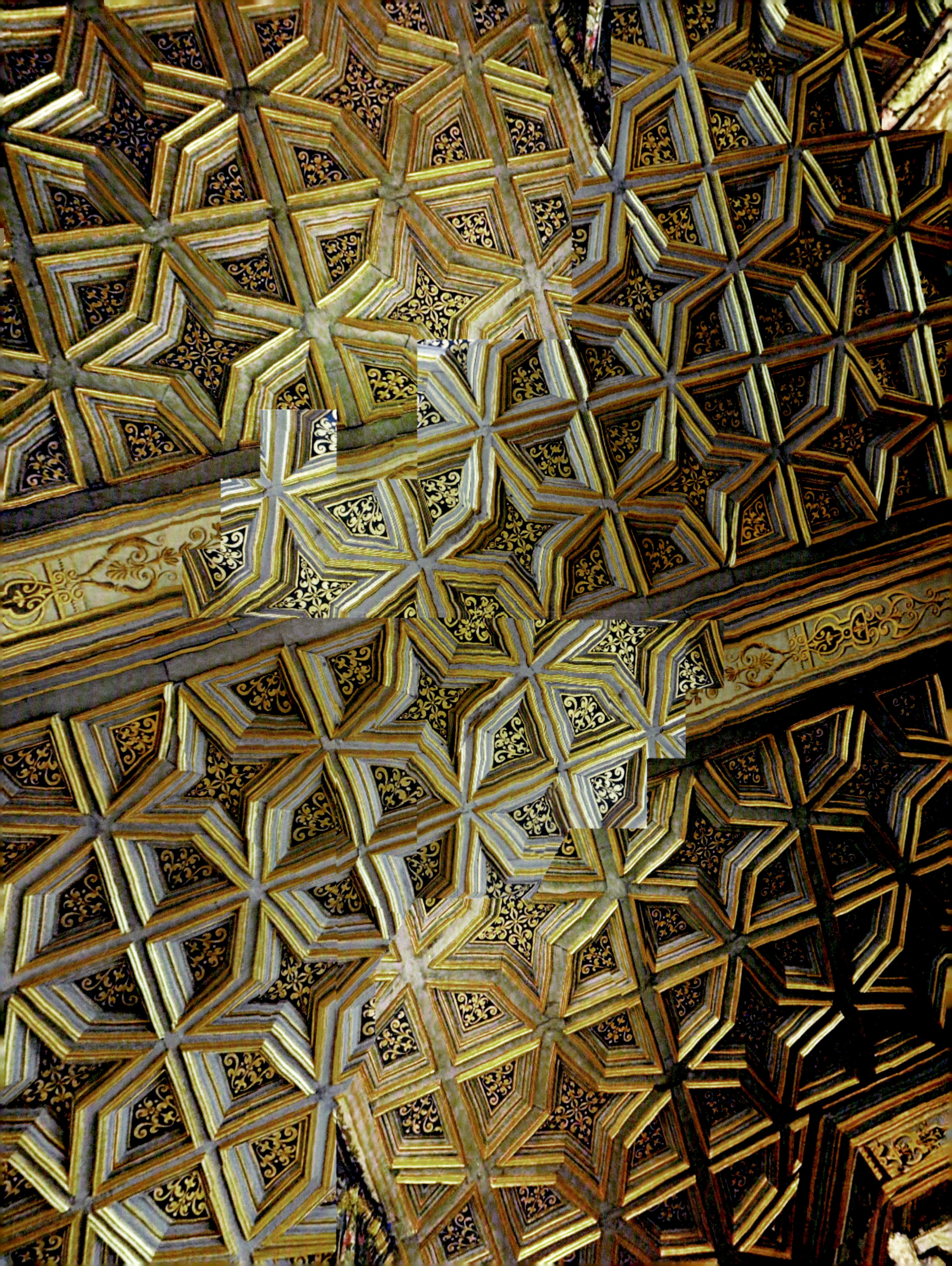

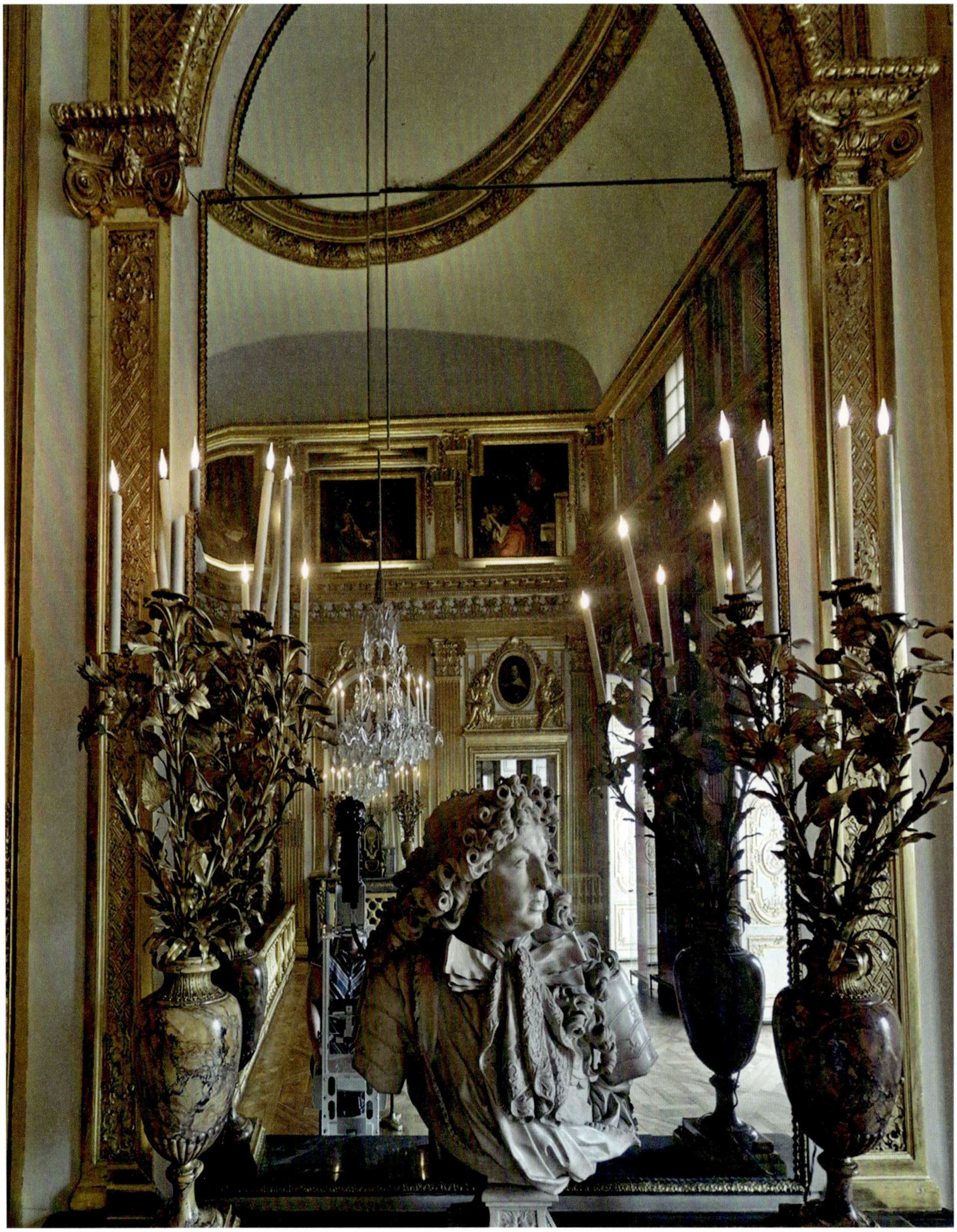

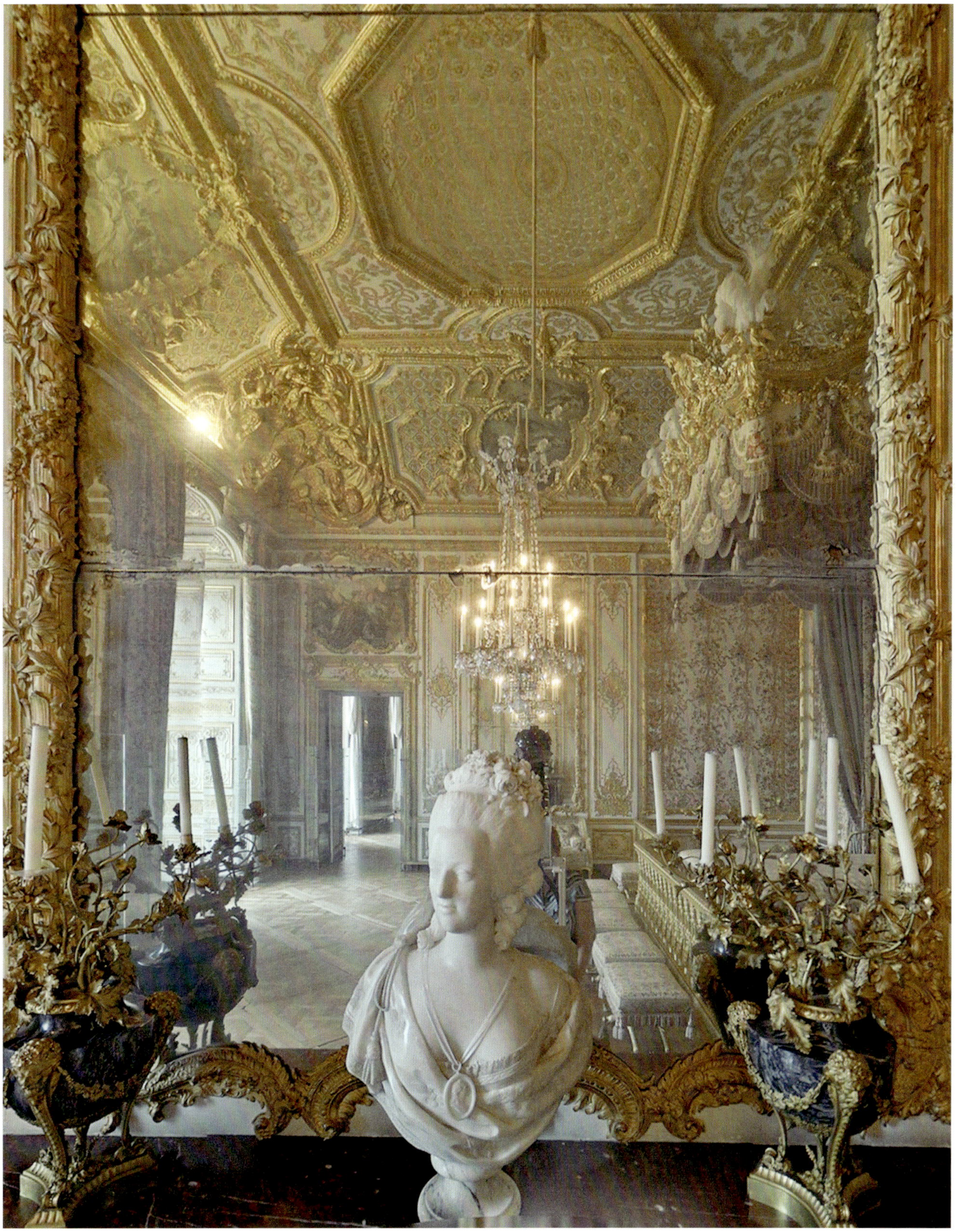

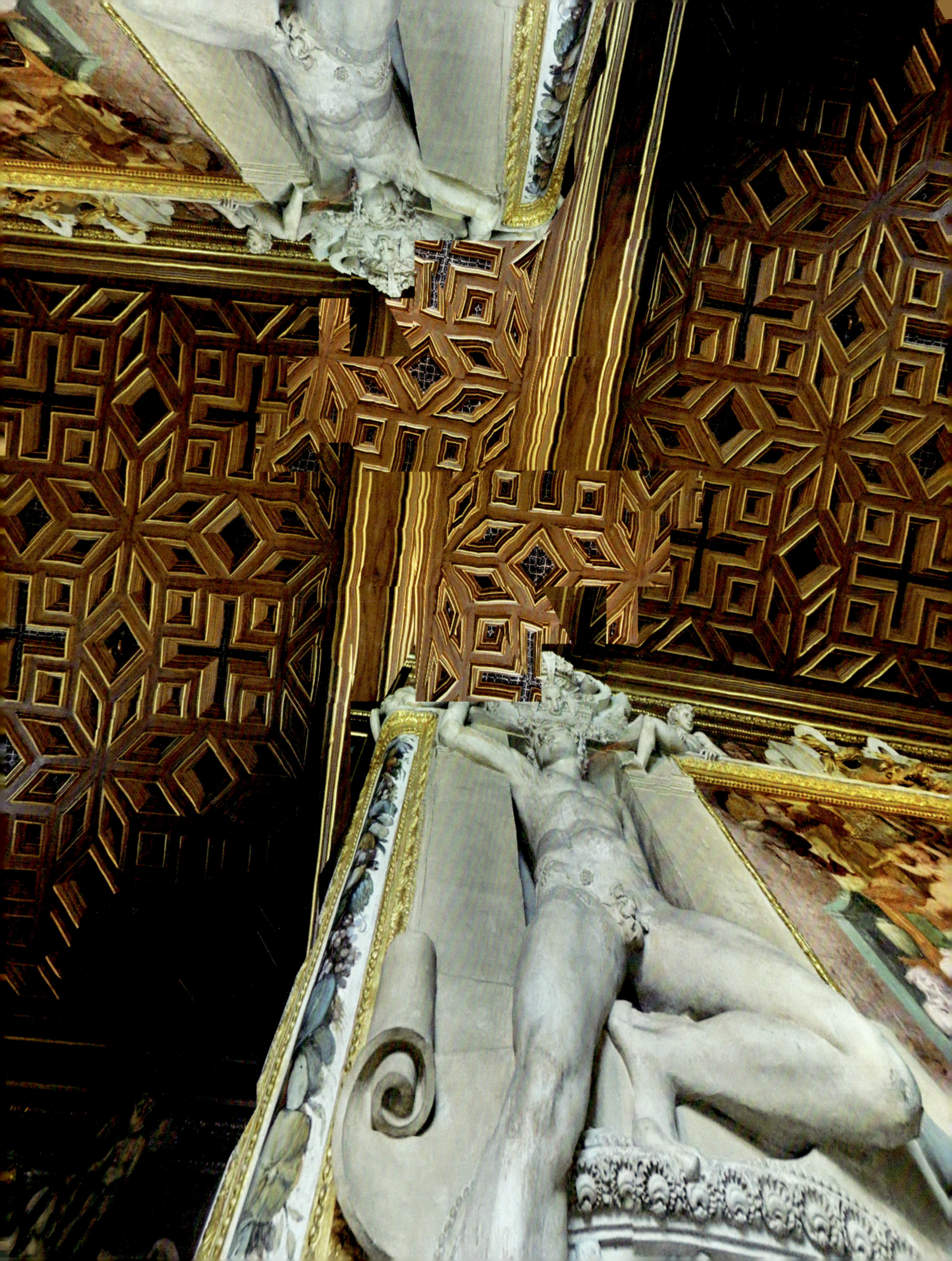

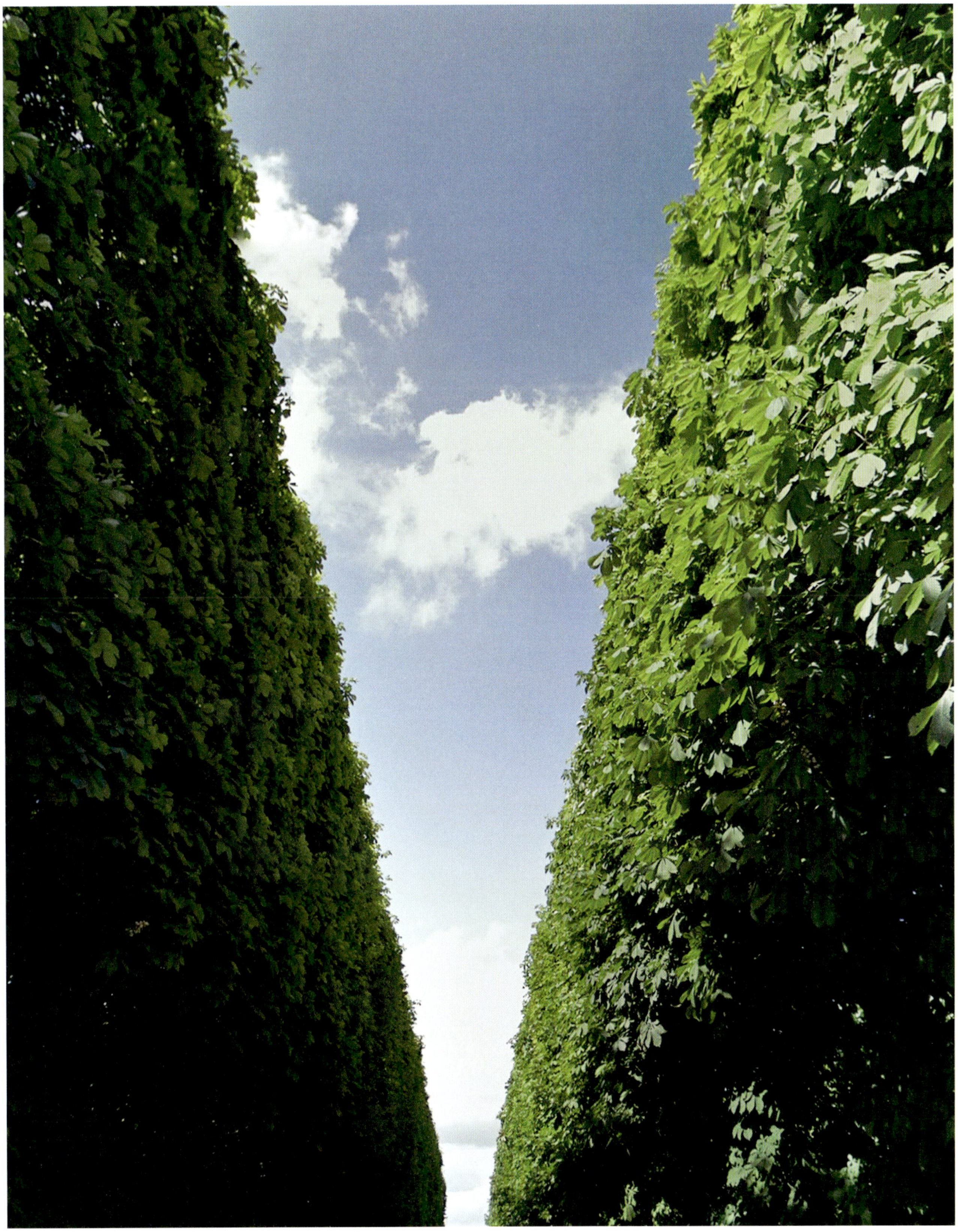

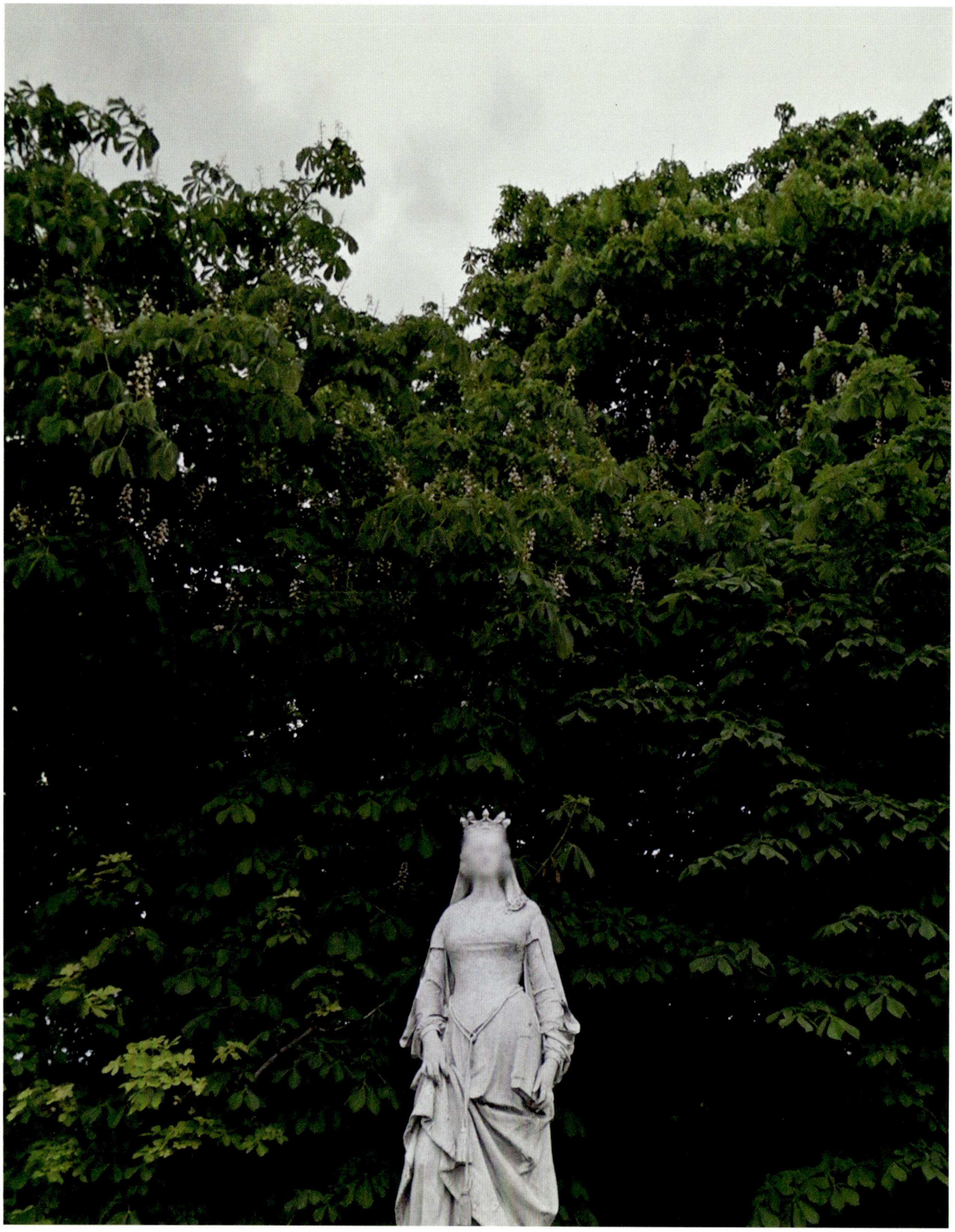

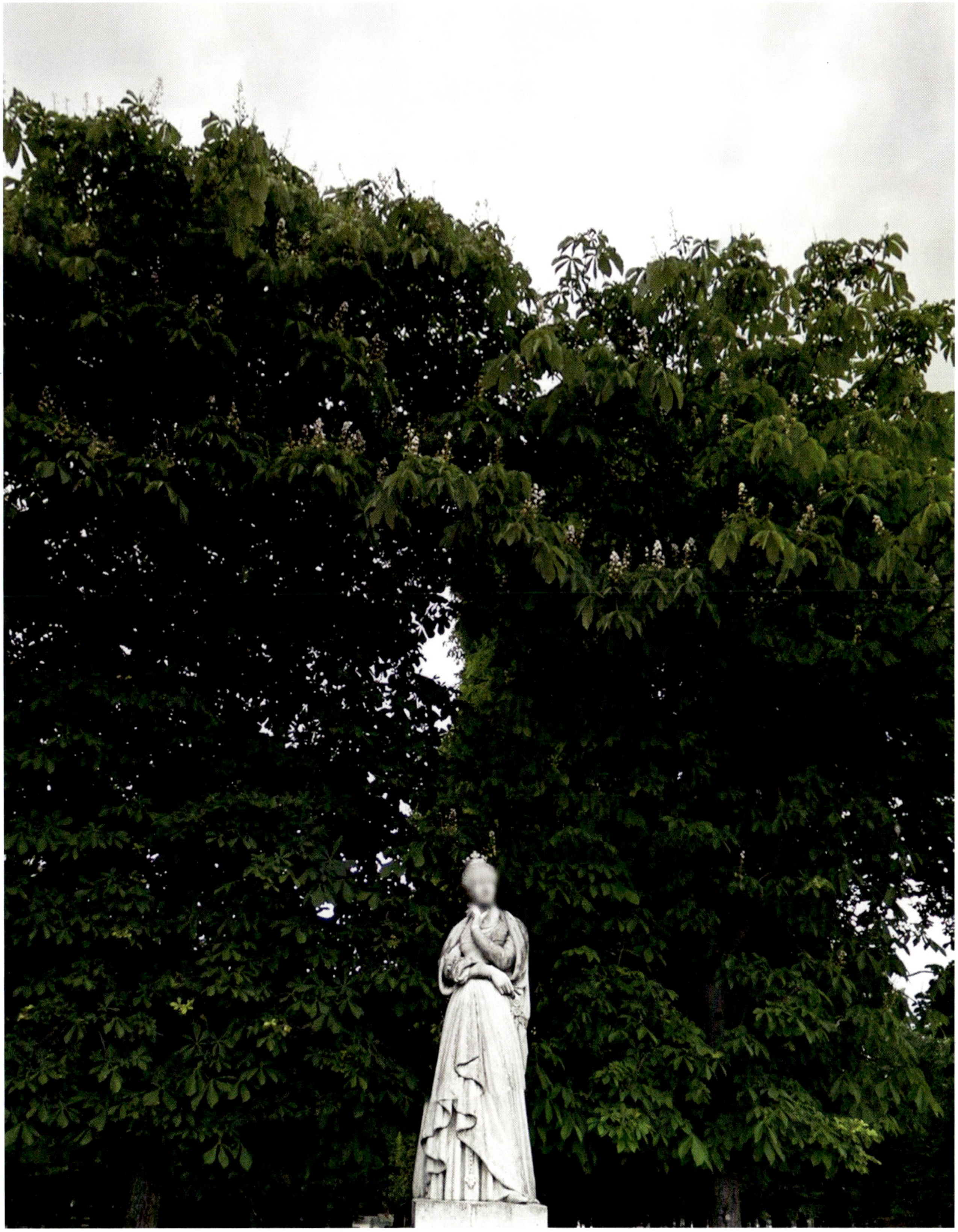

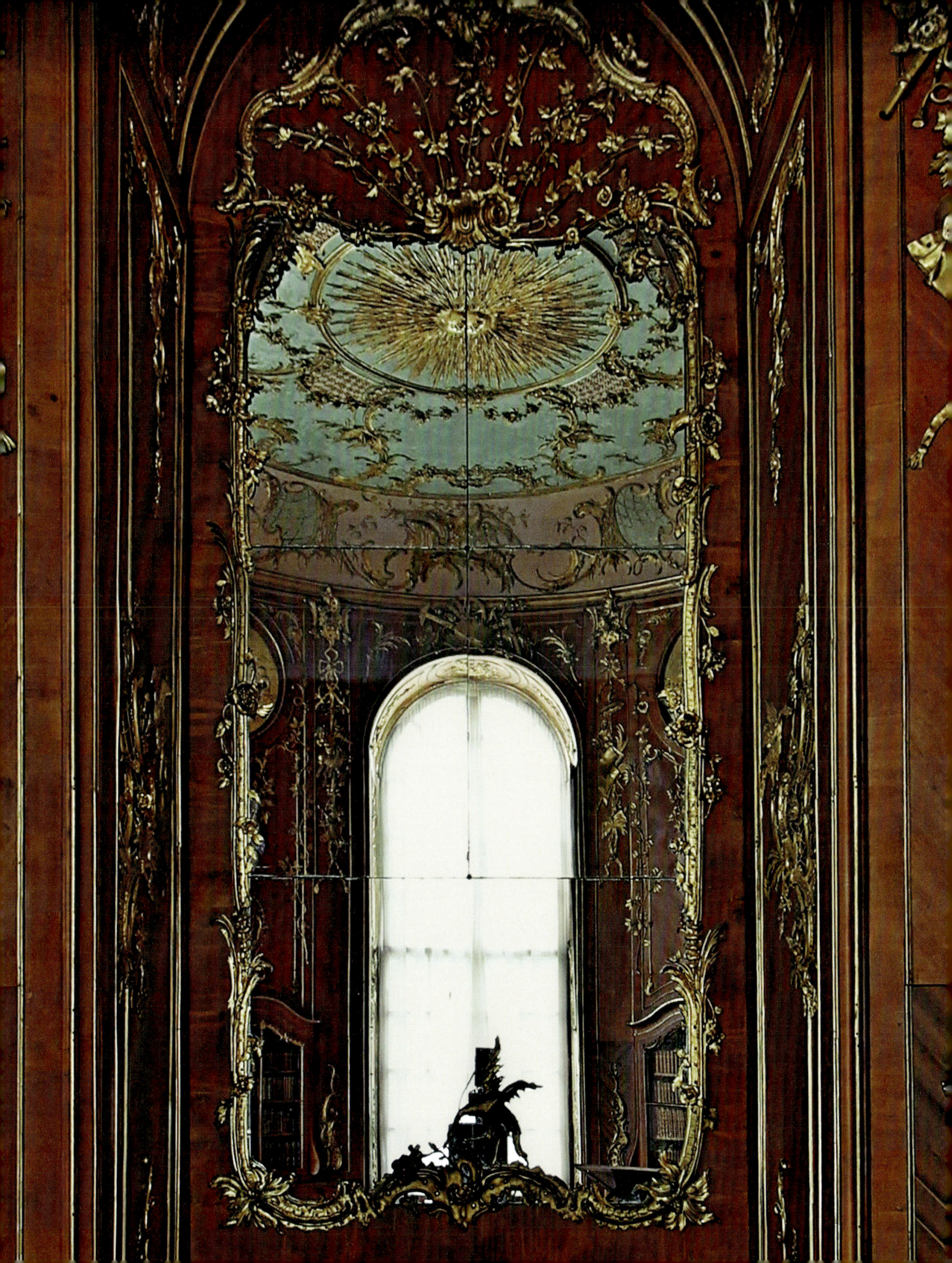

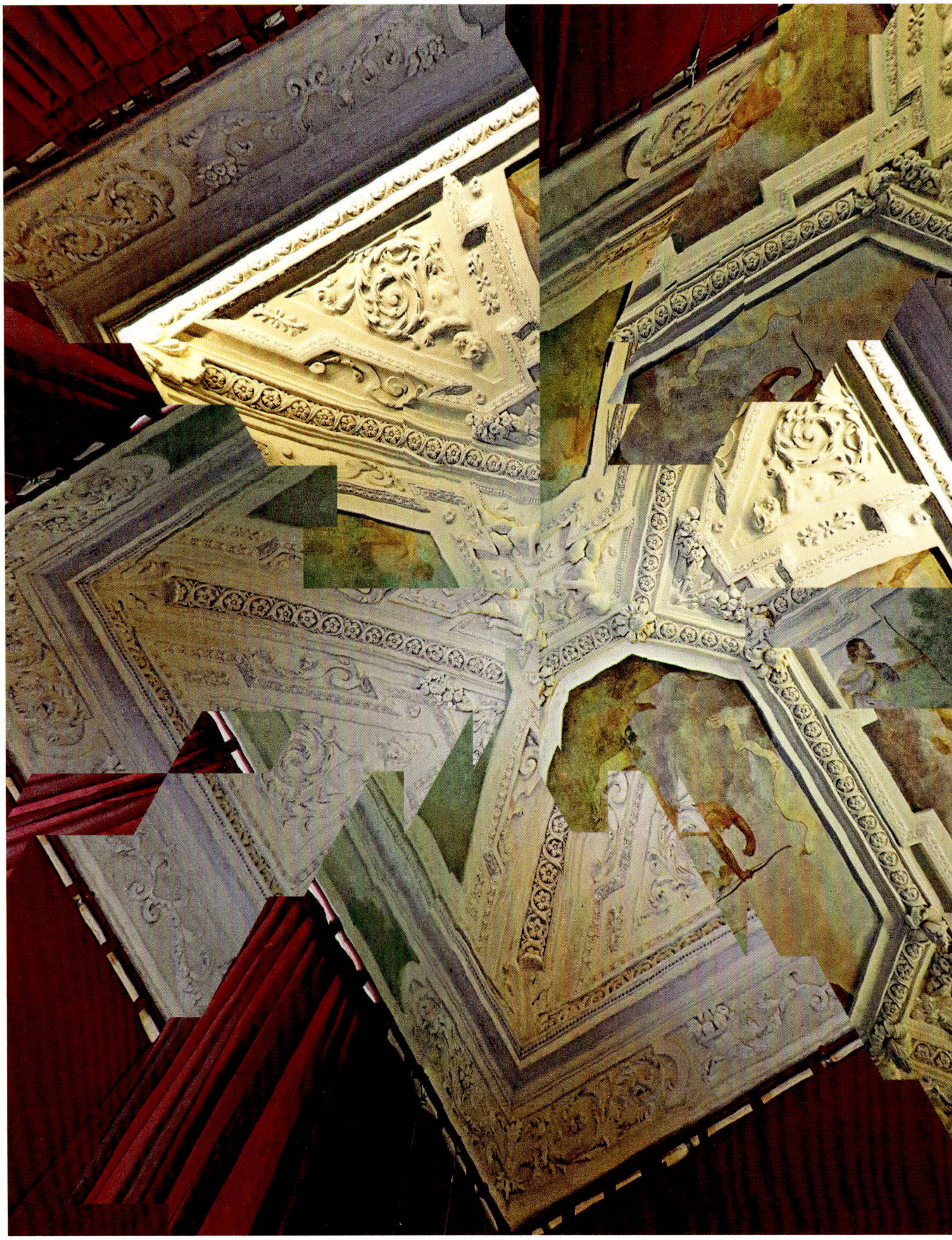

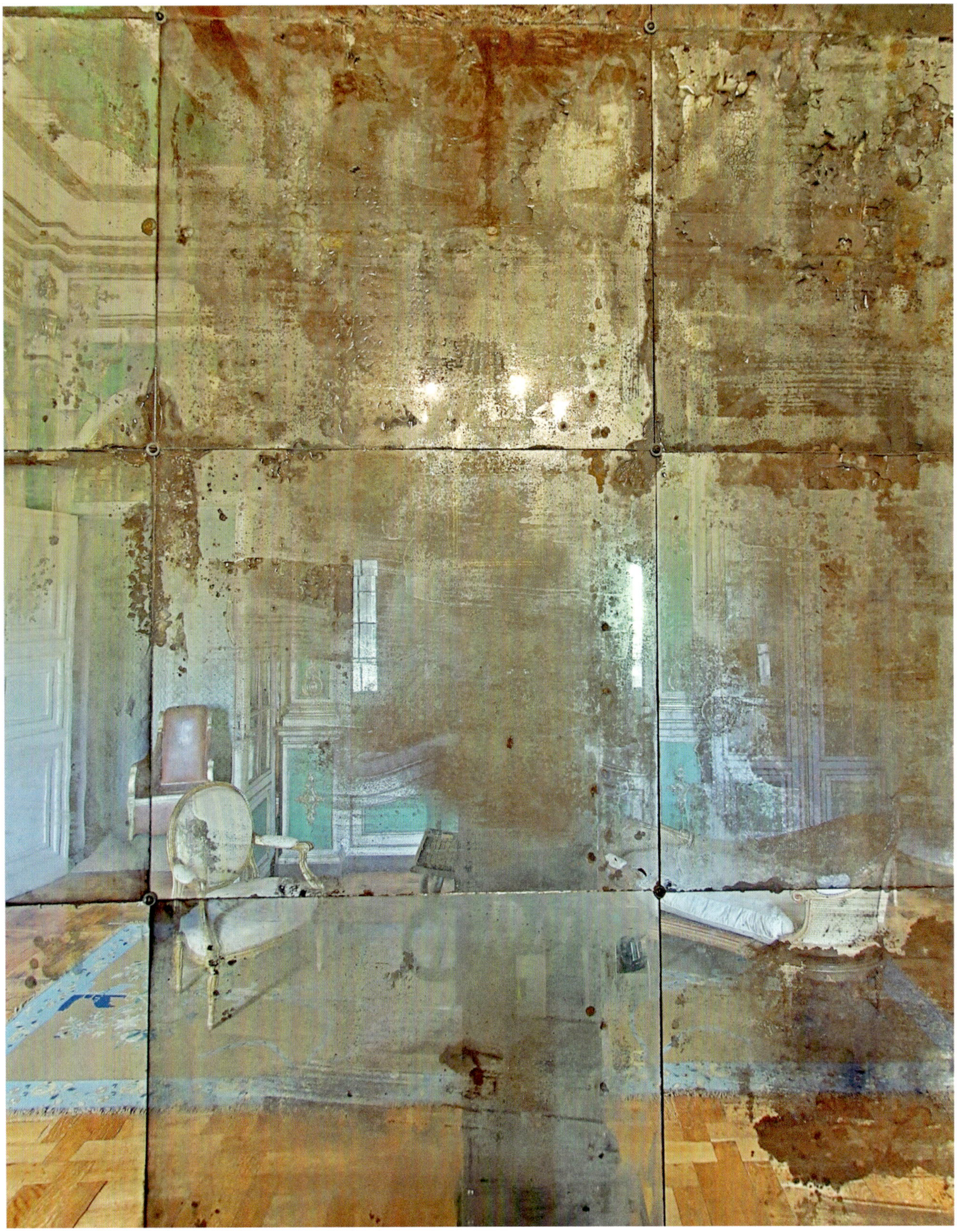

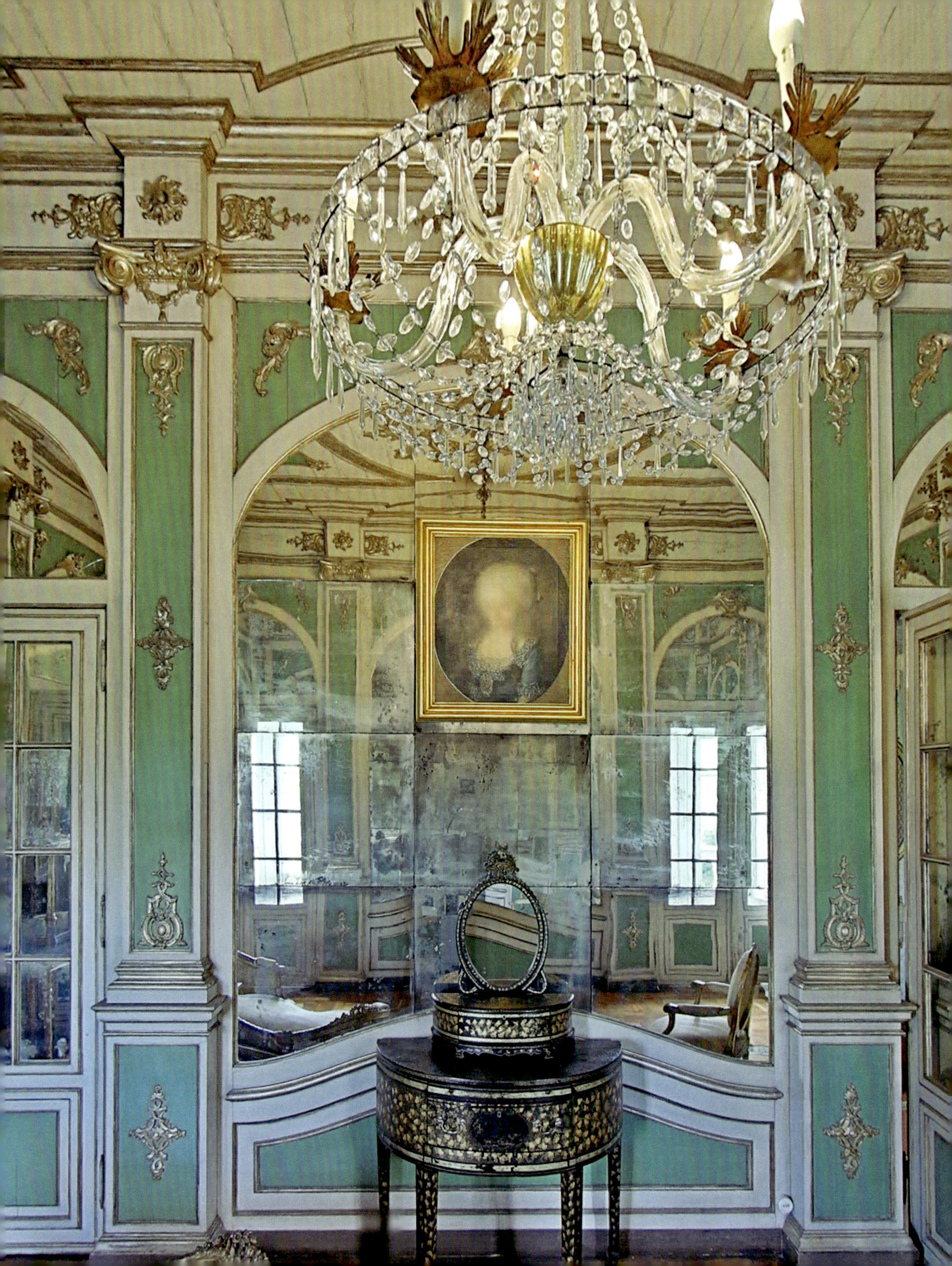

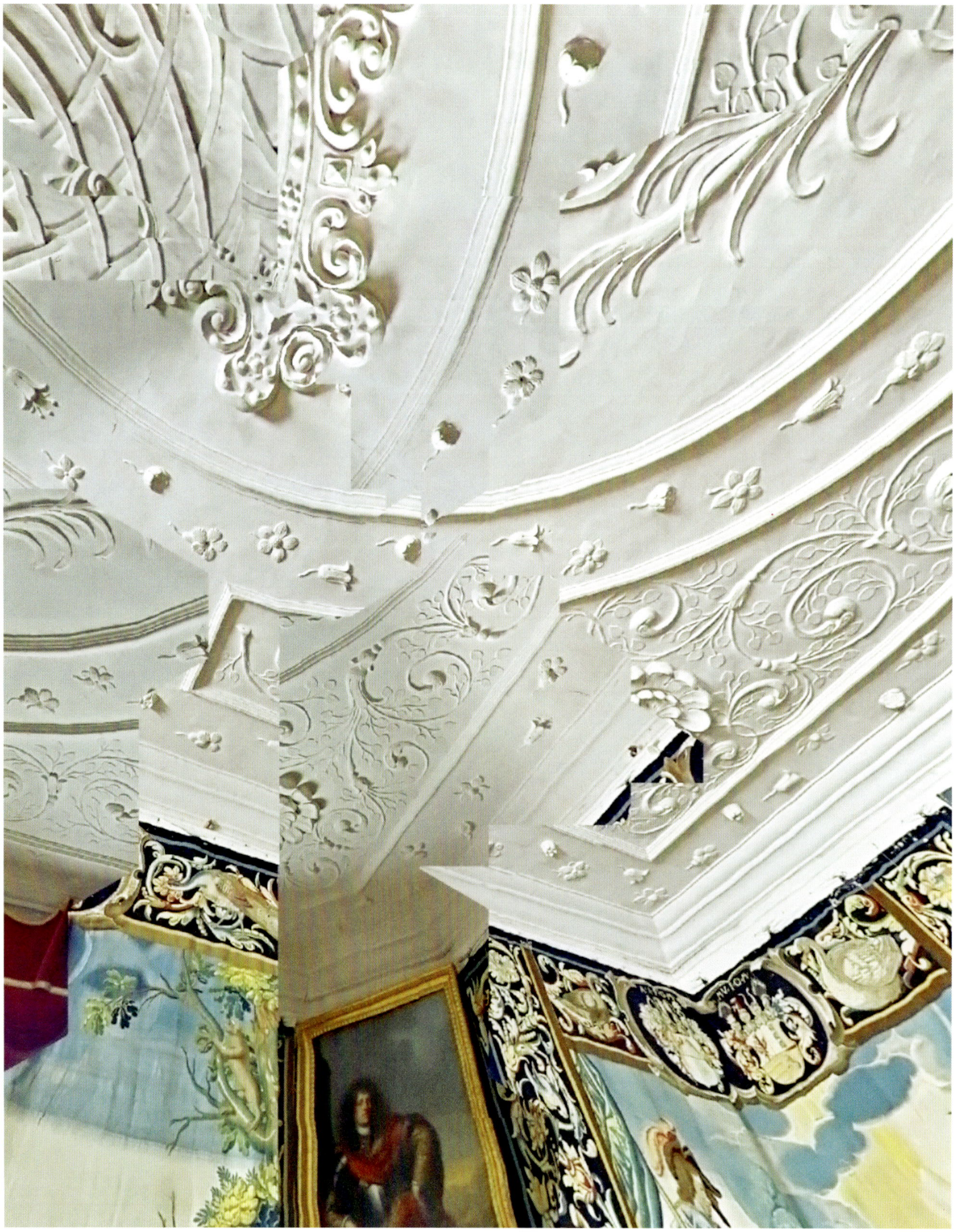

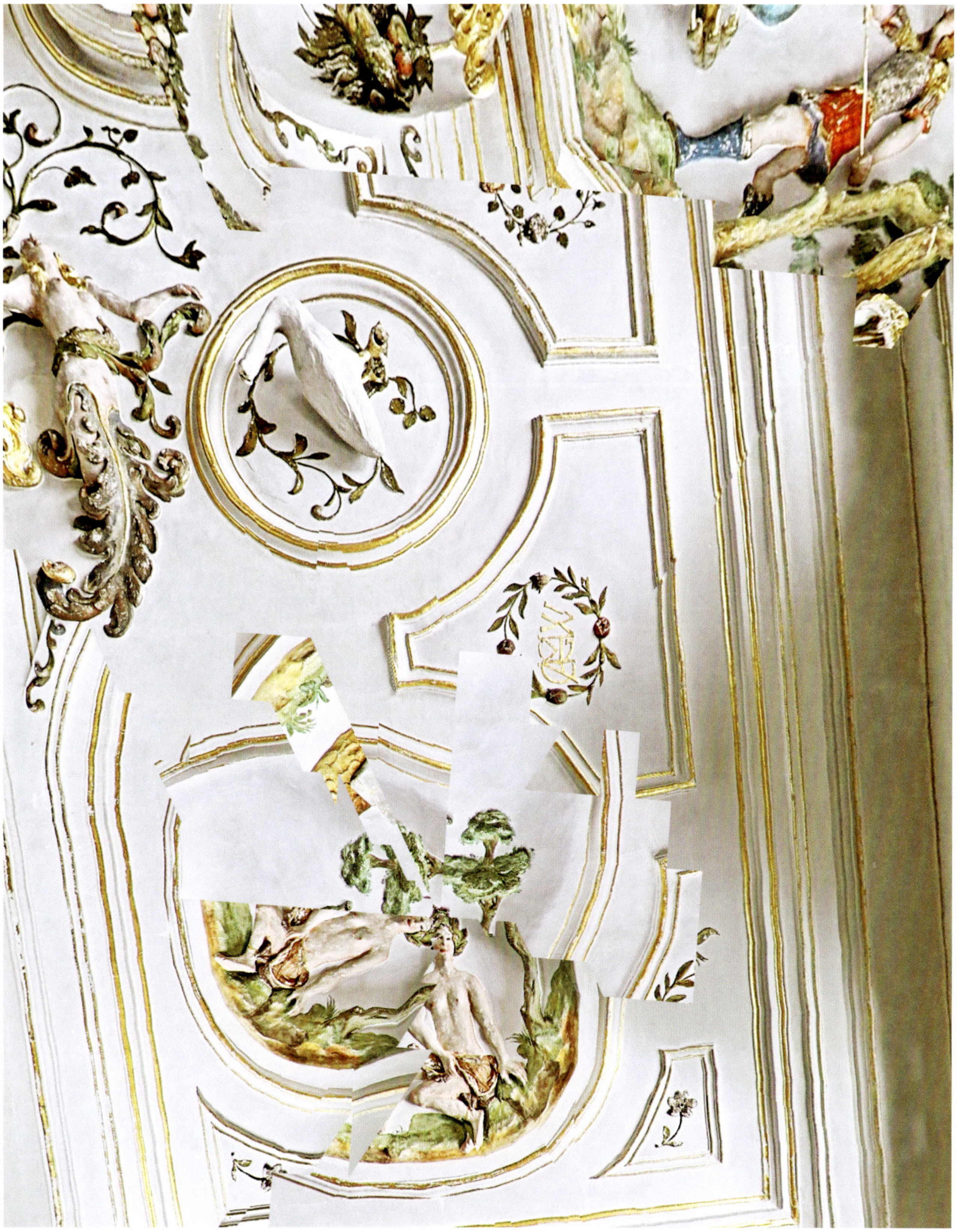

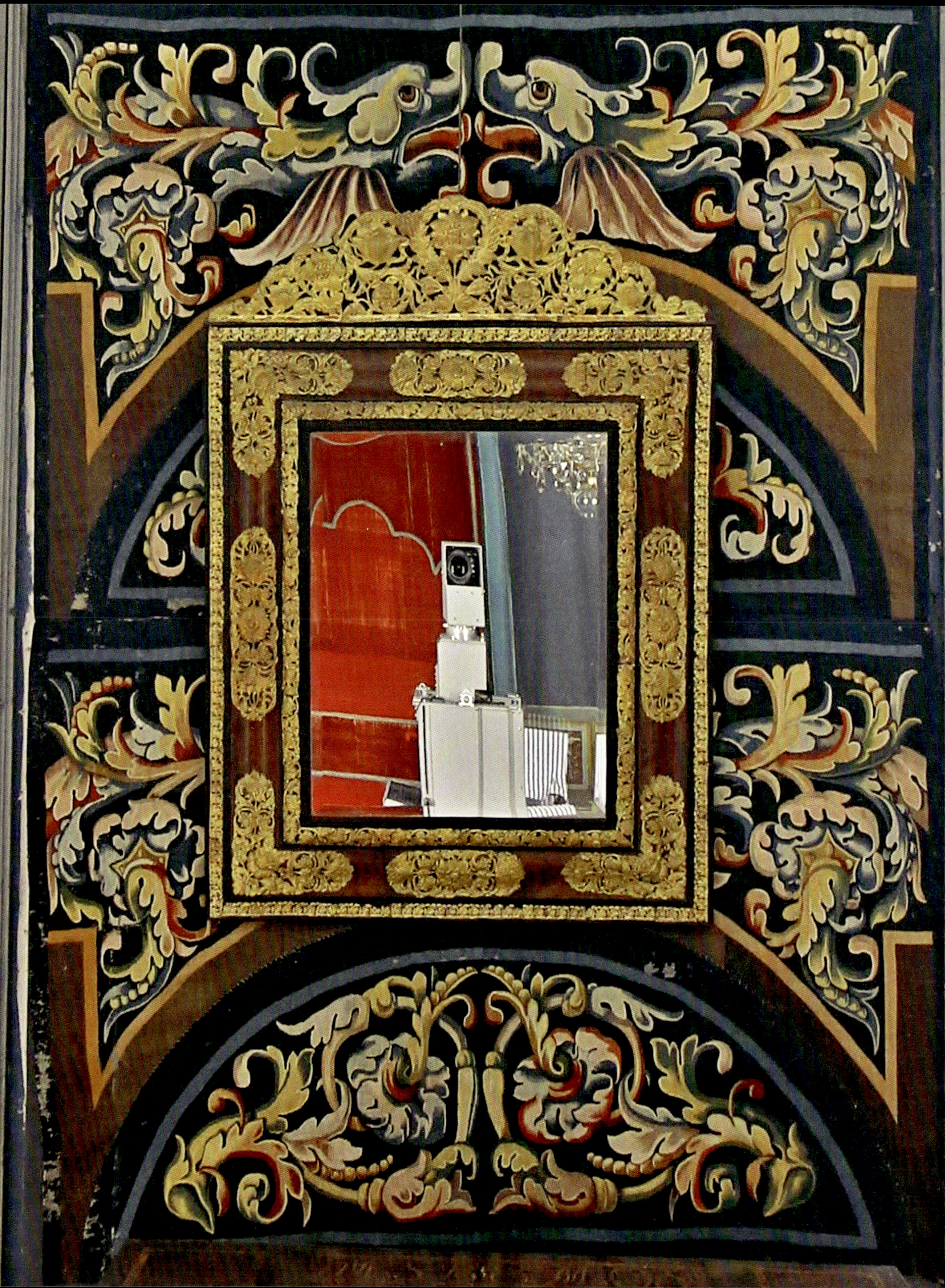

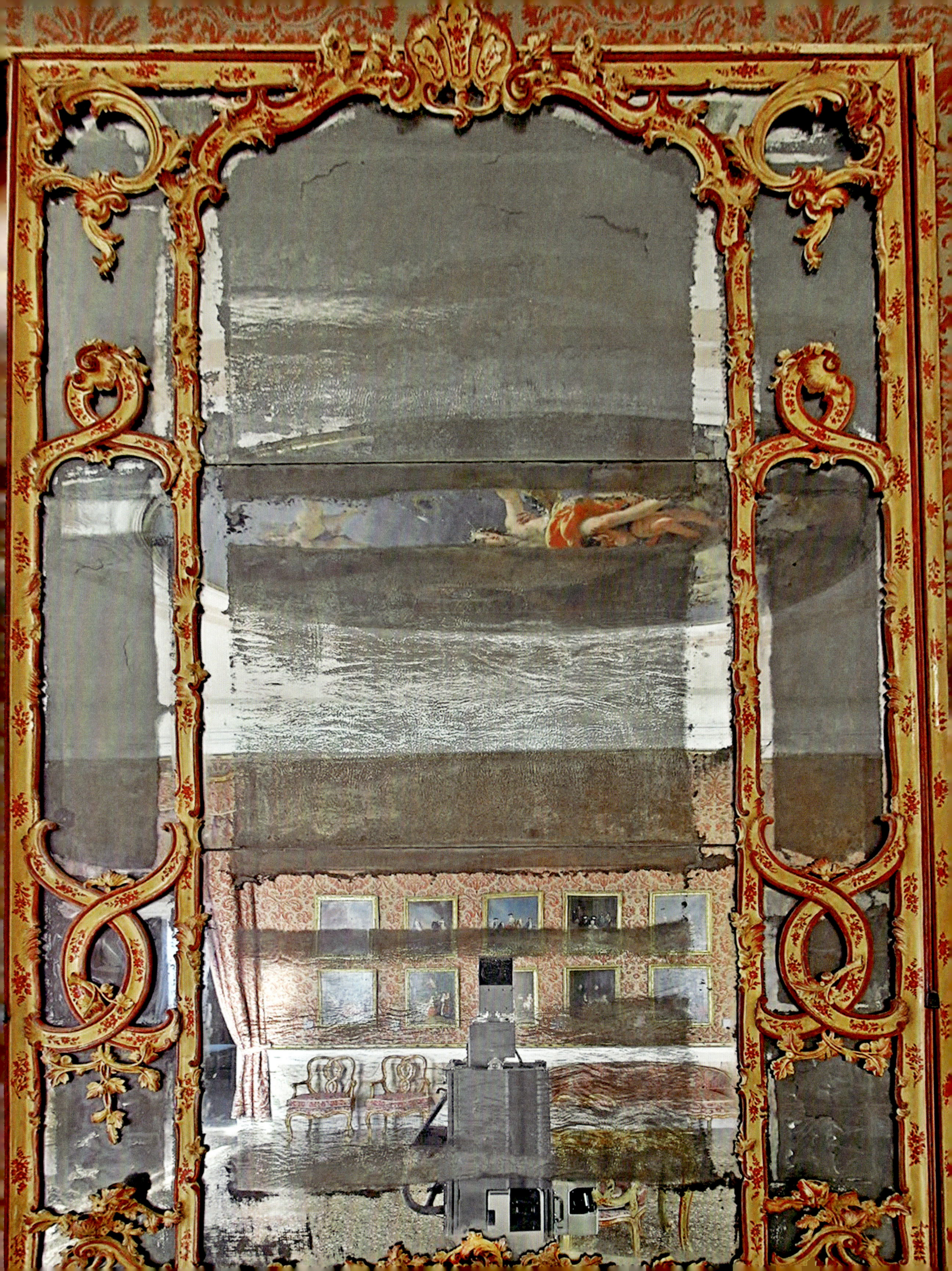

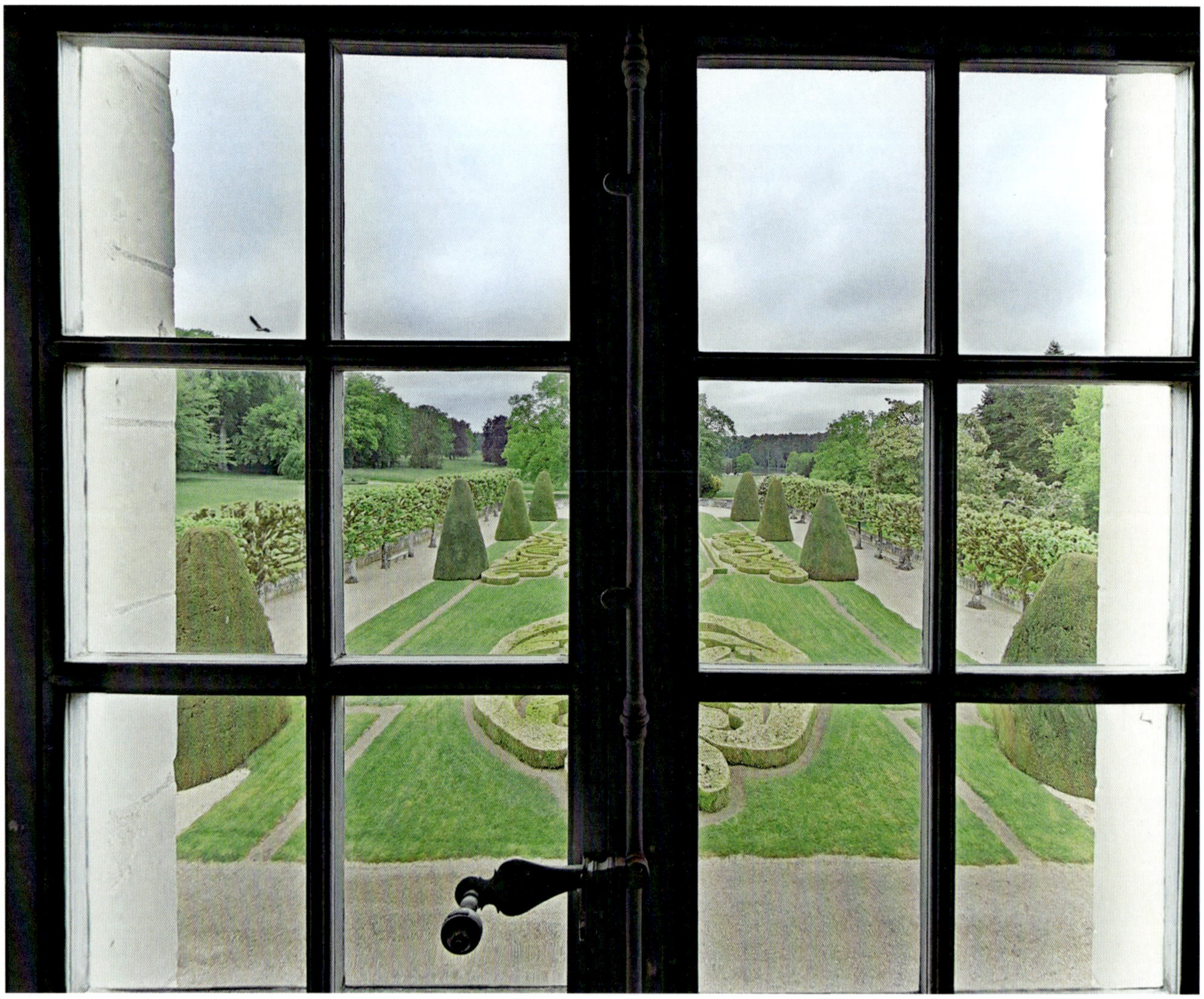

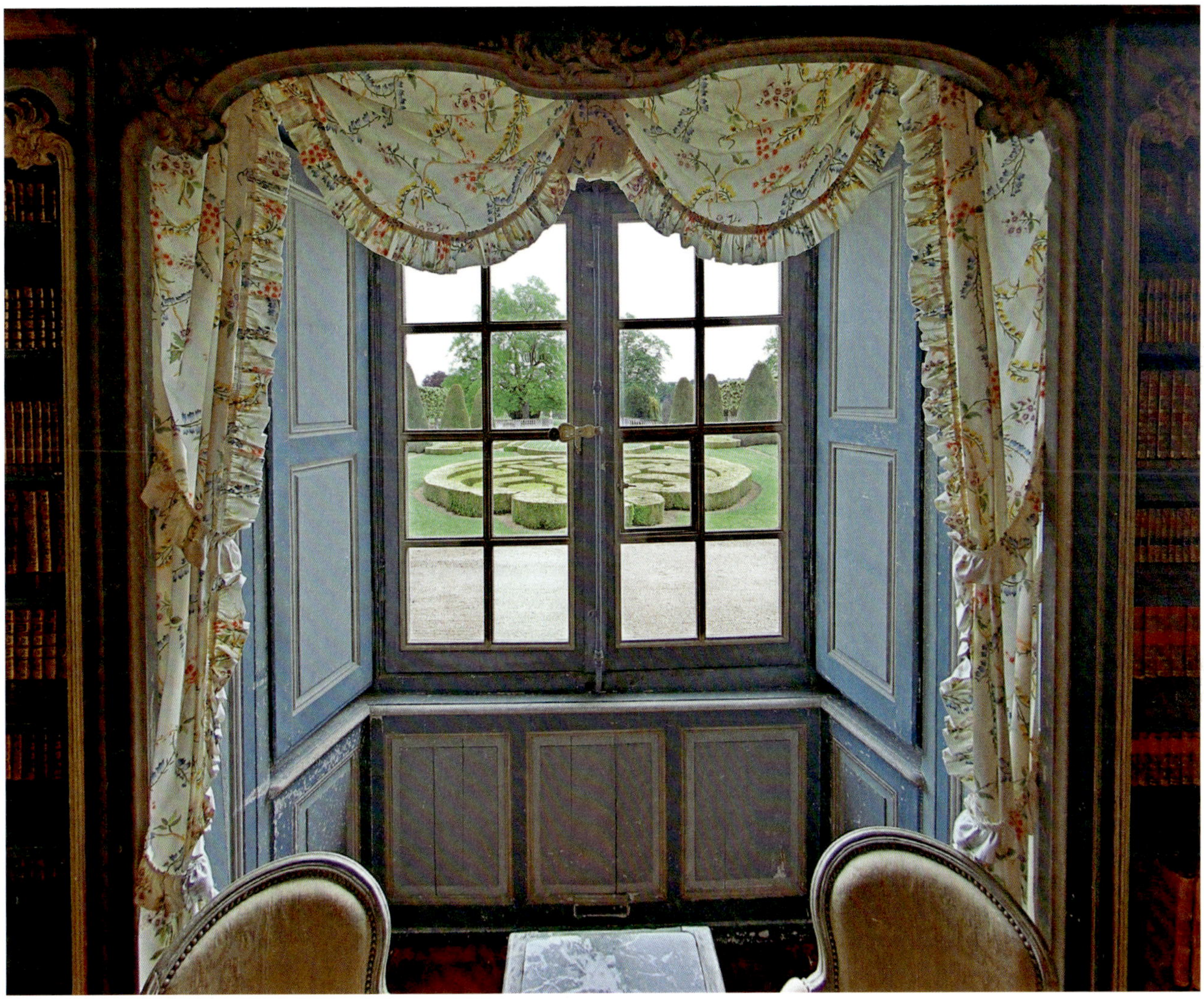

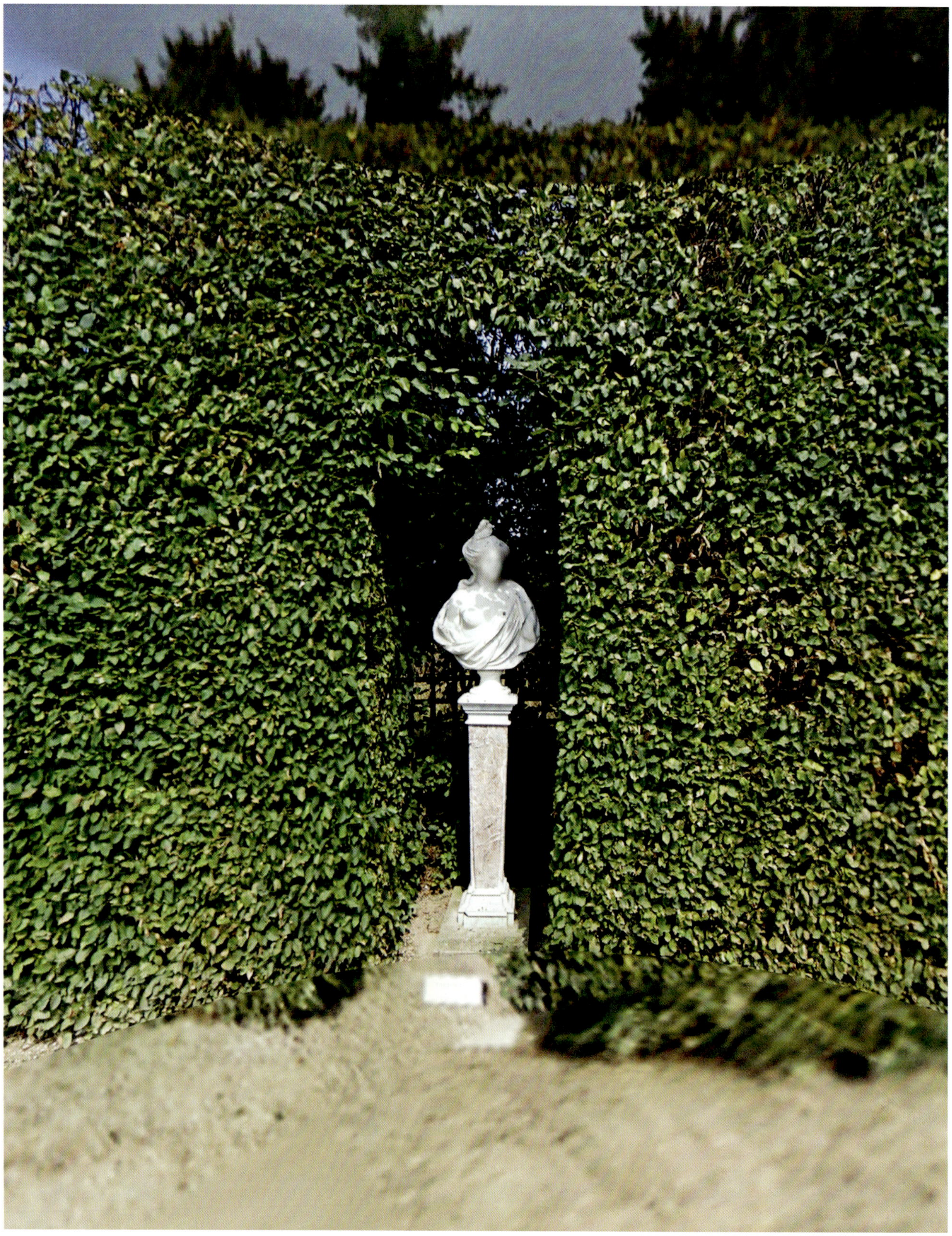

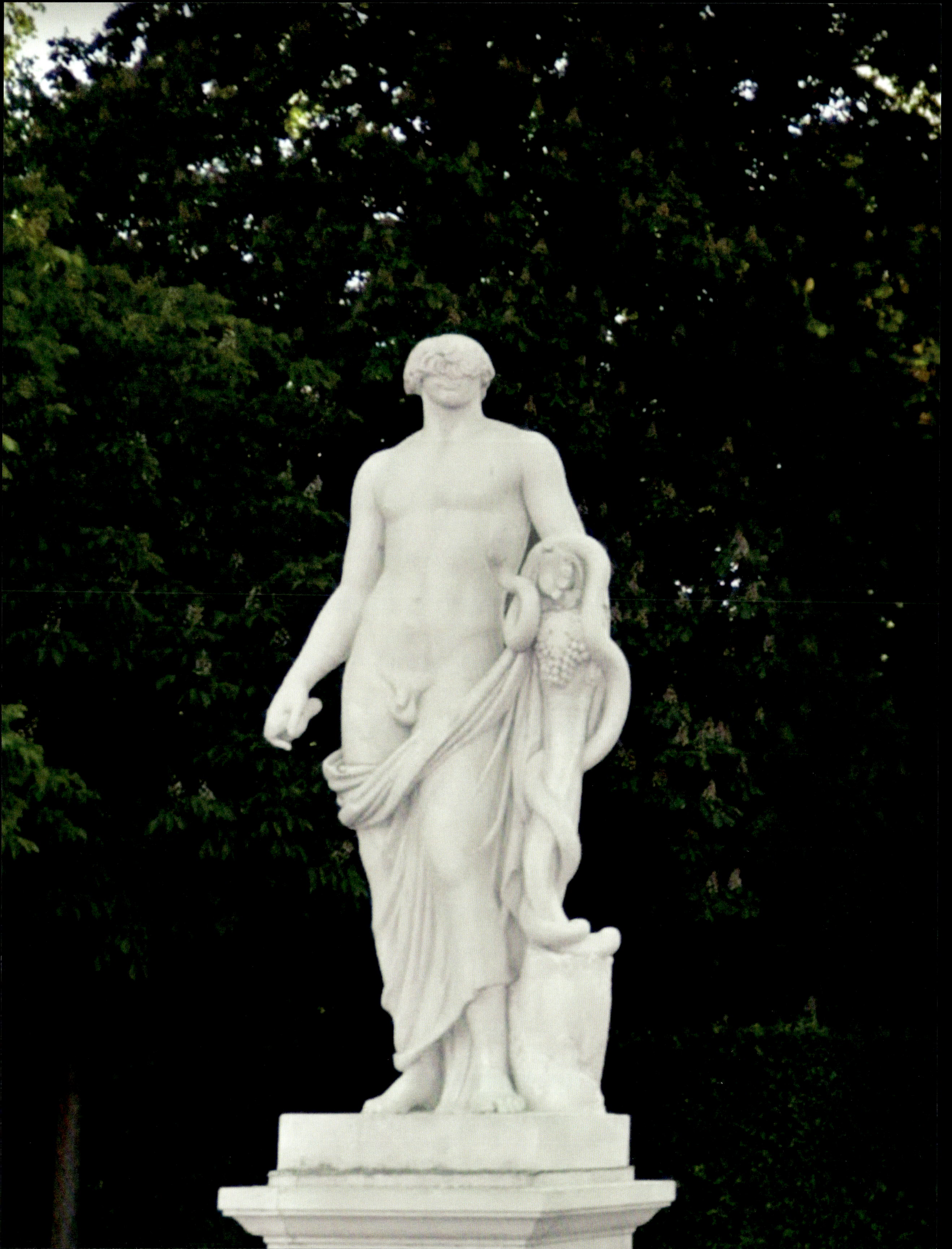

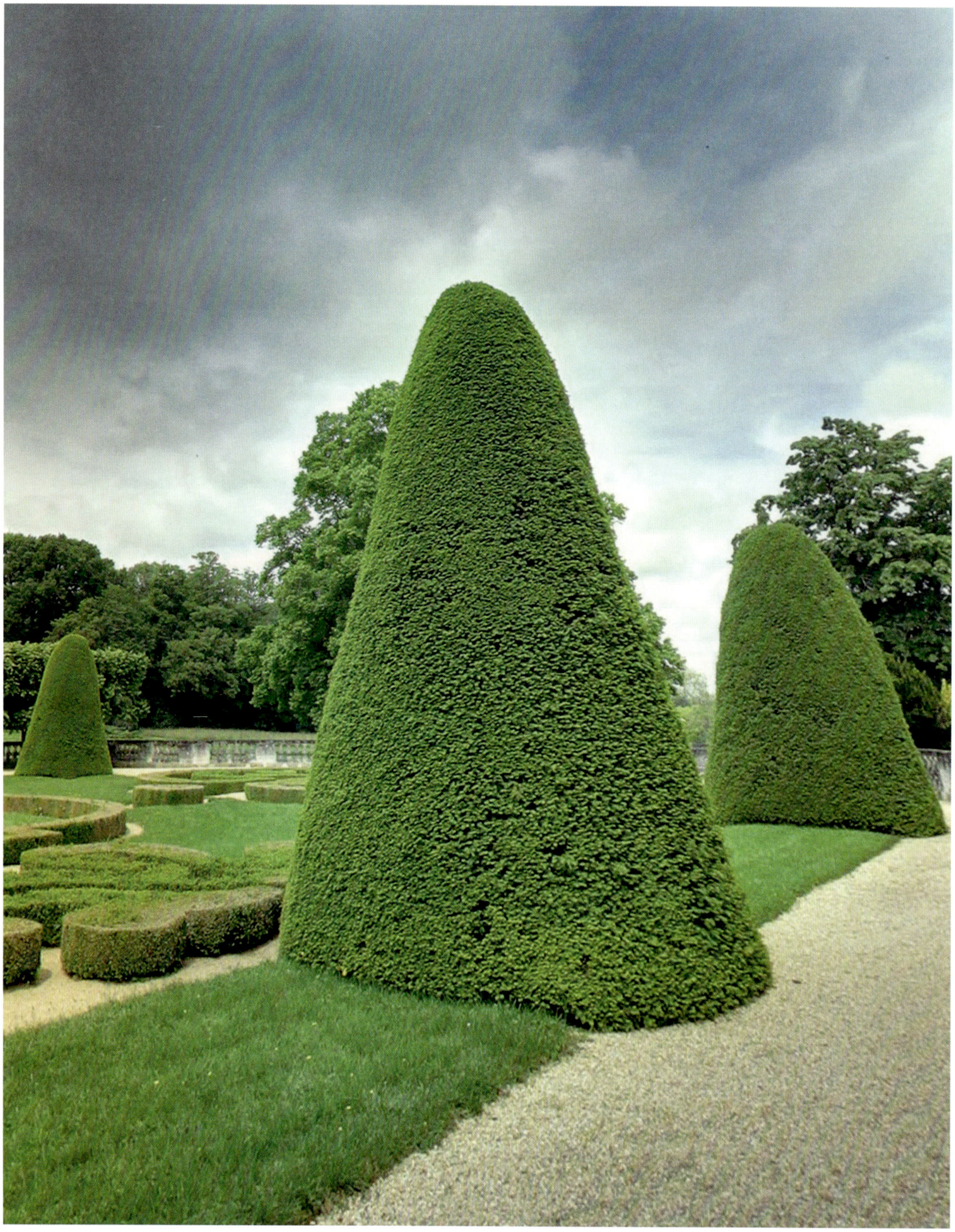

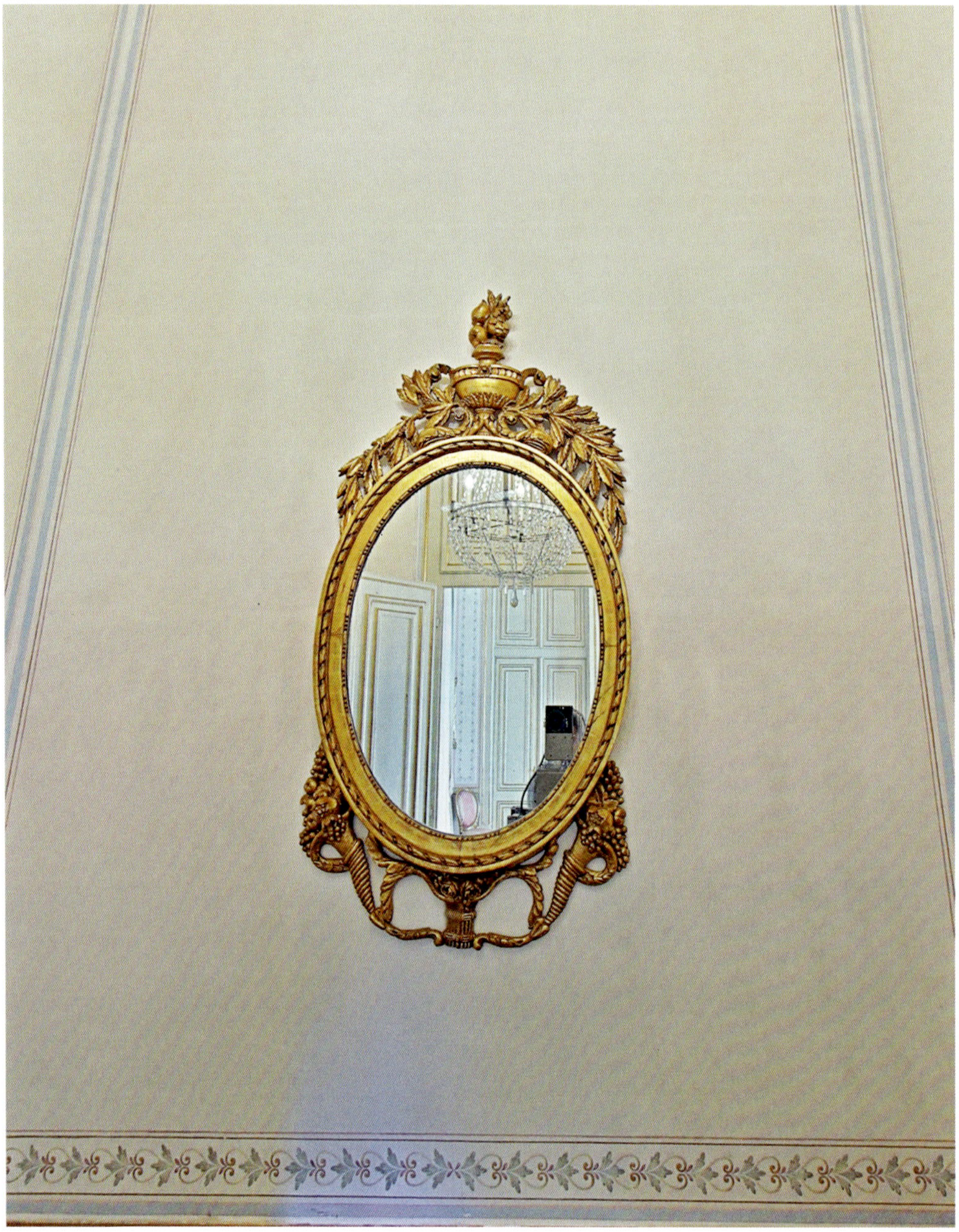

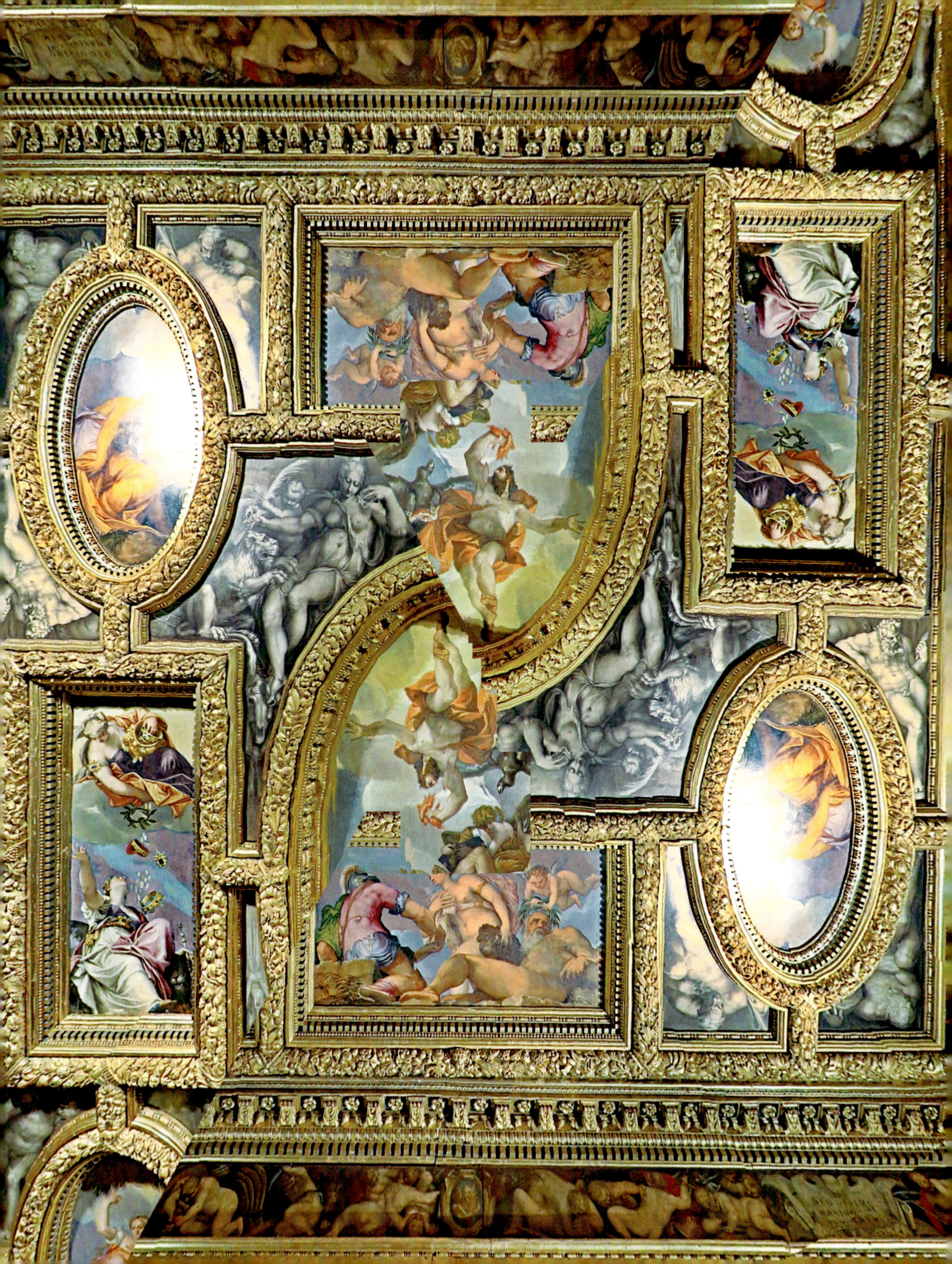

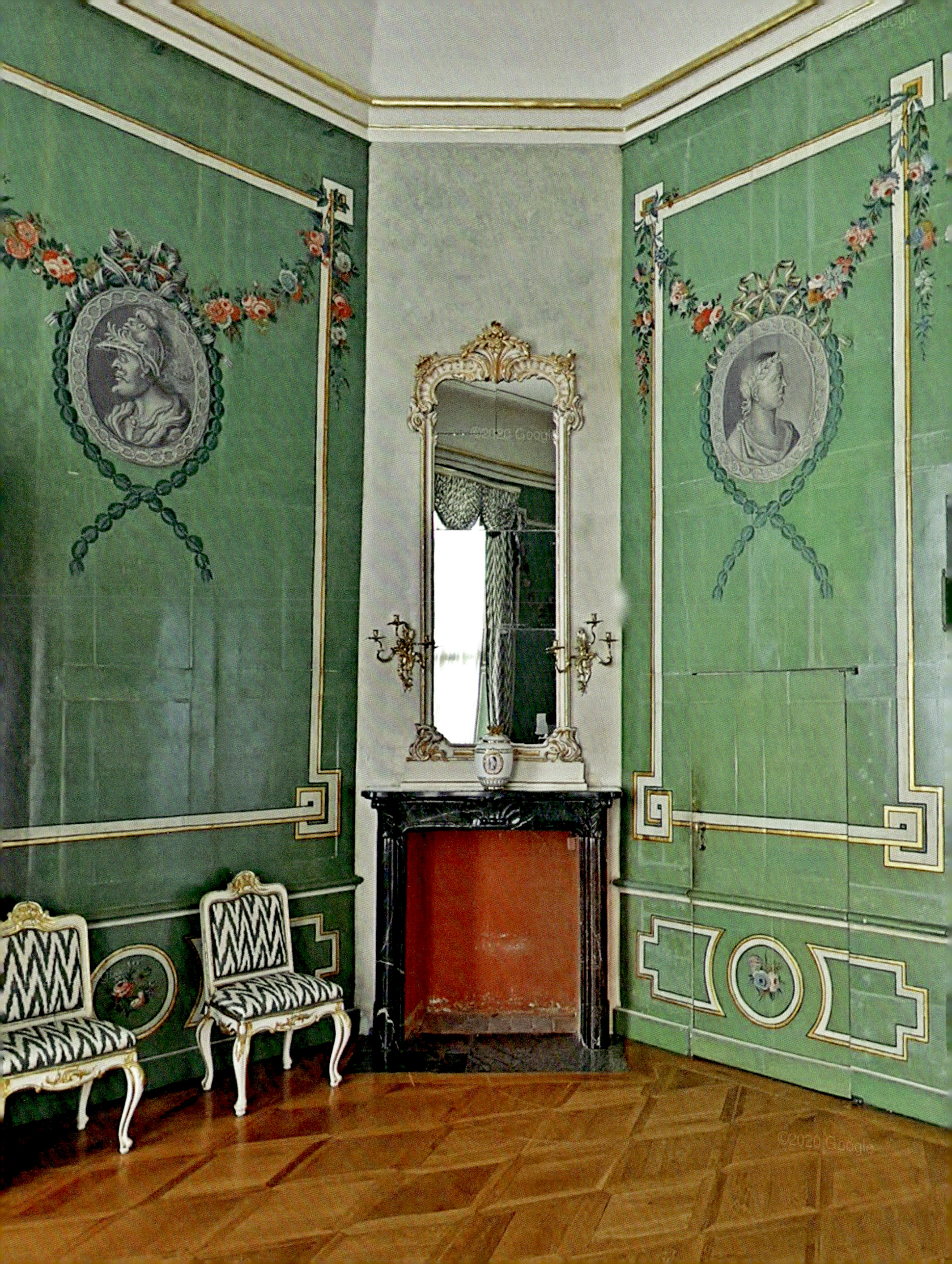
©2020 Google

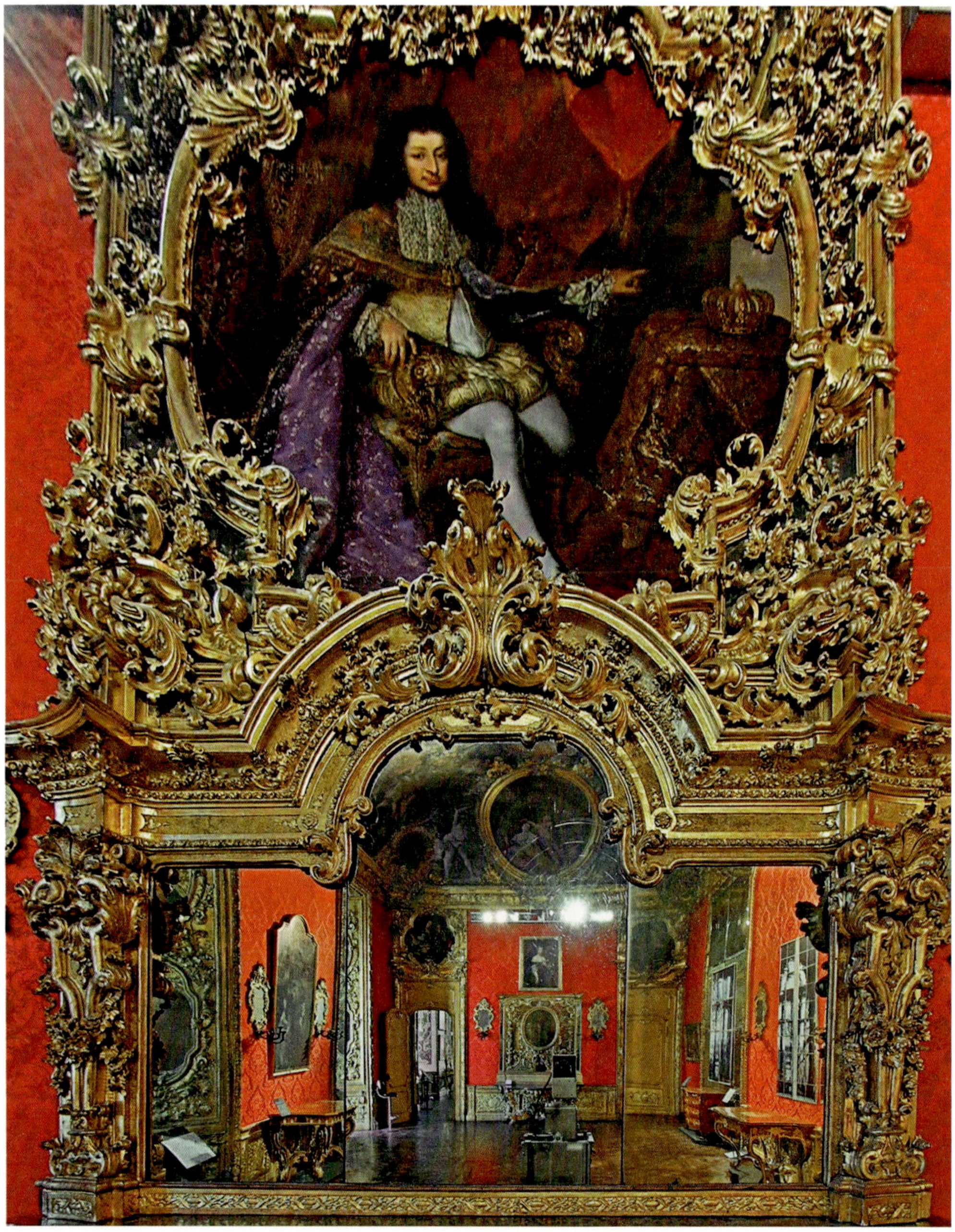

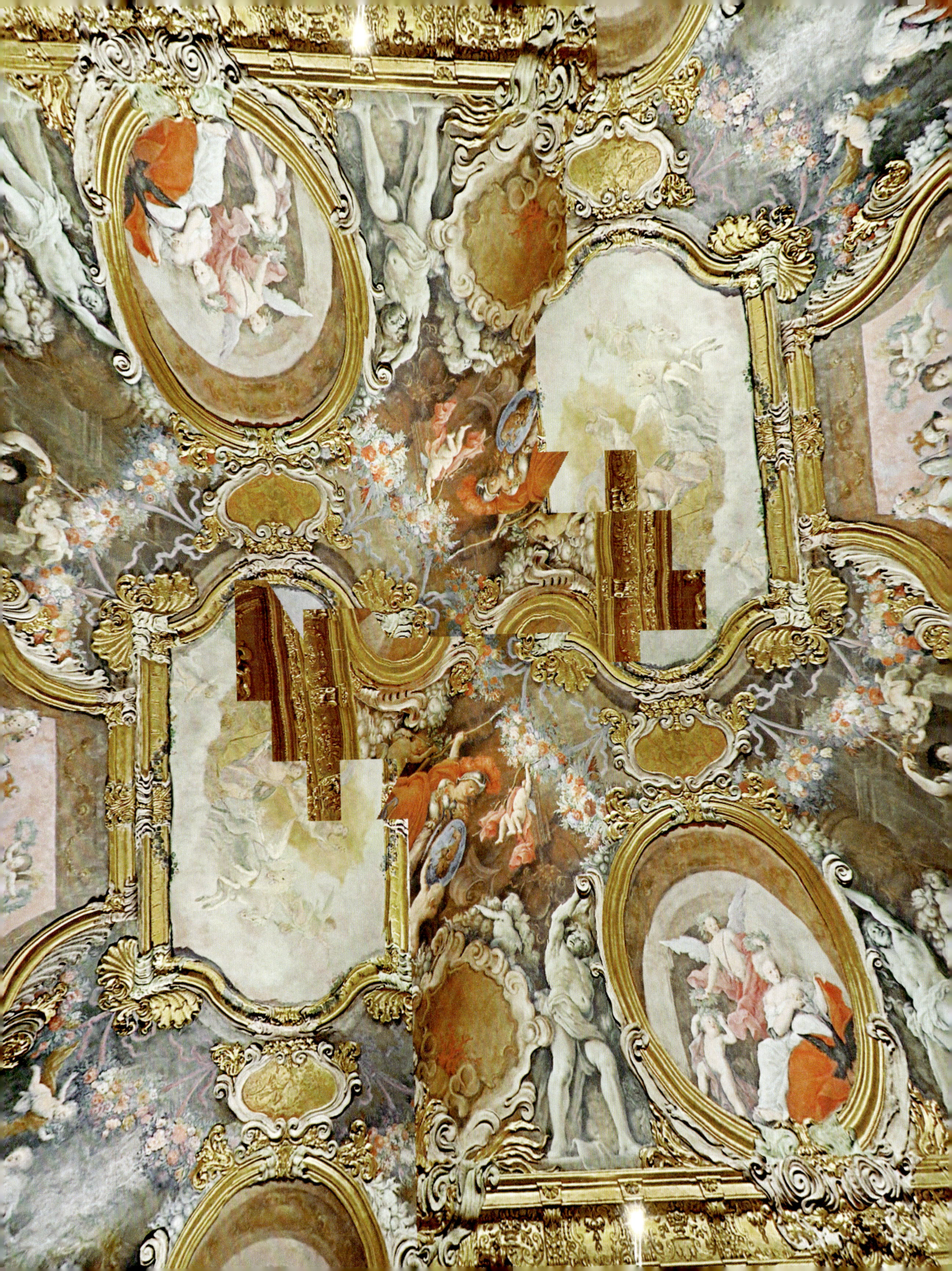

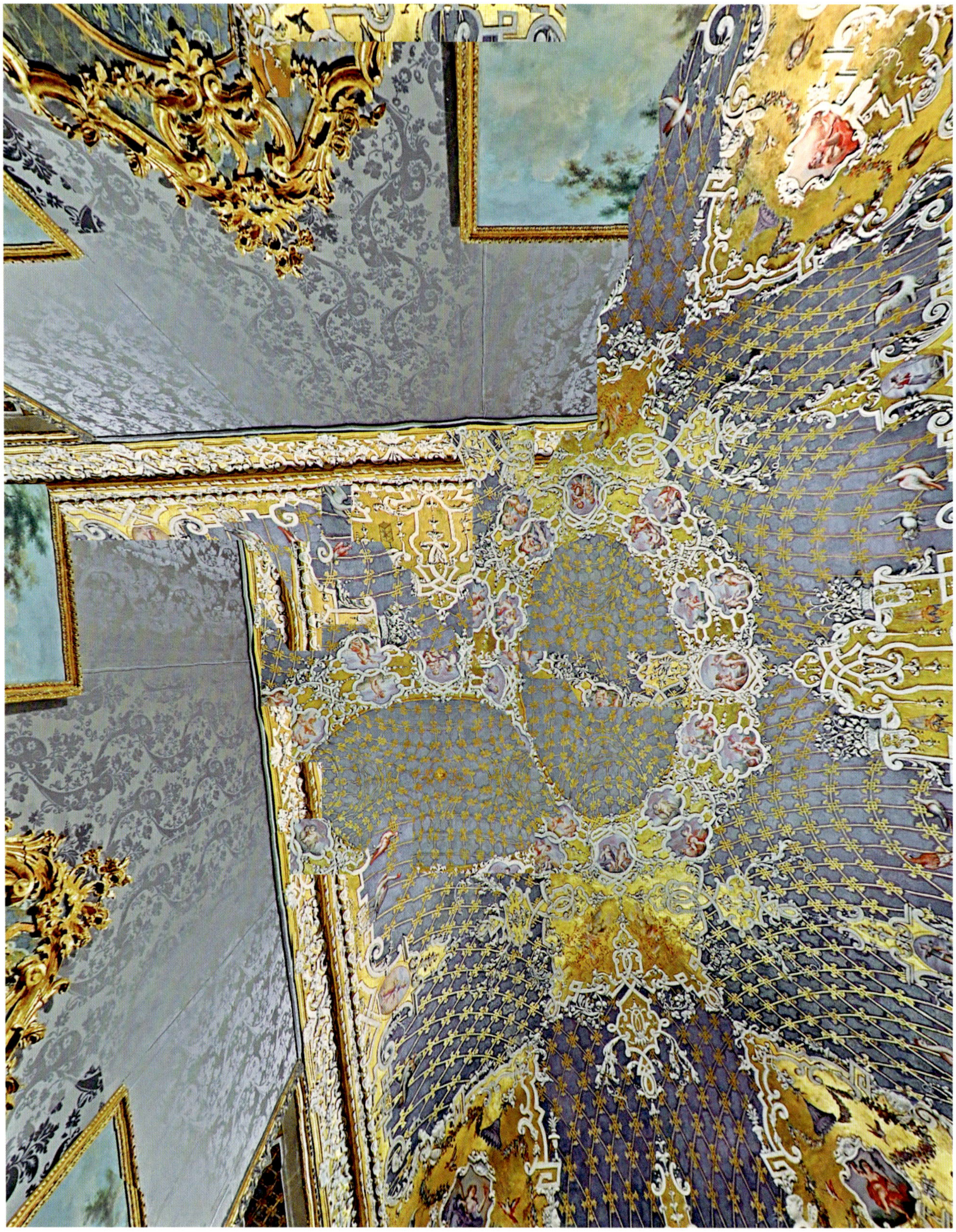

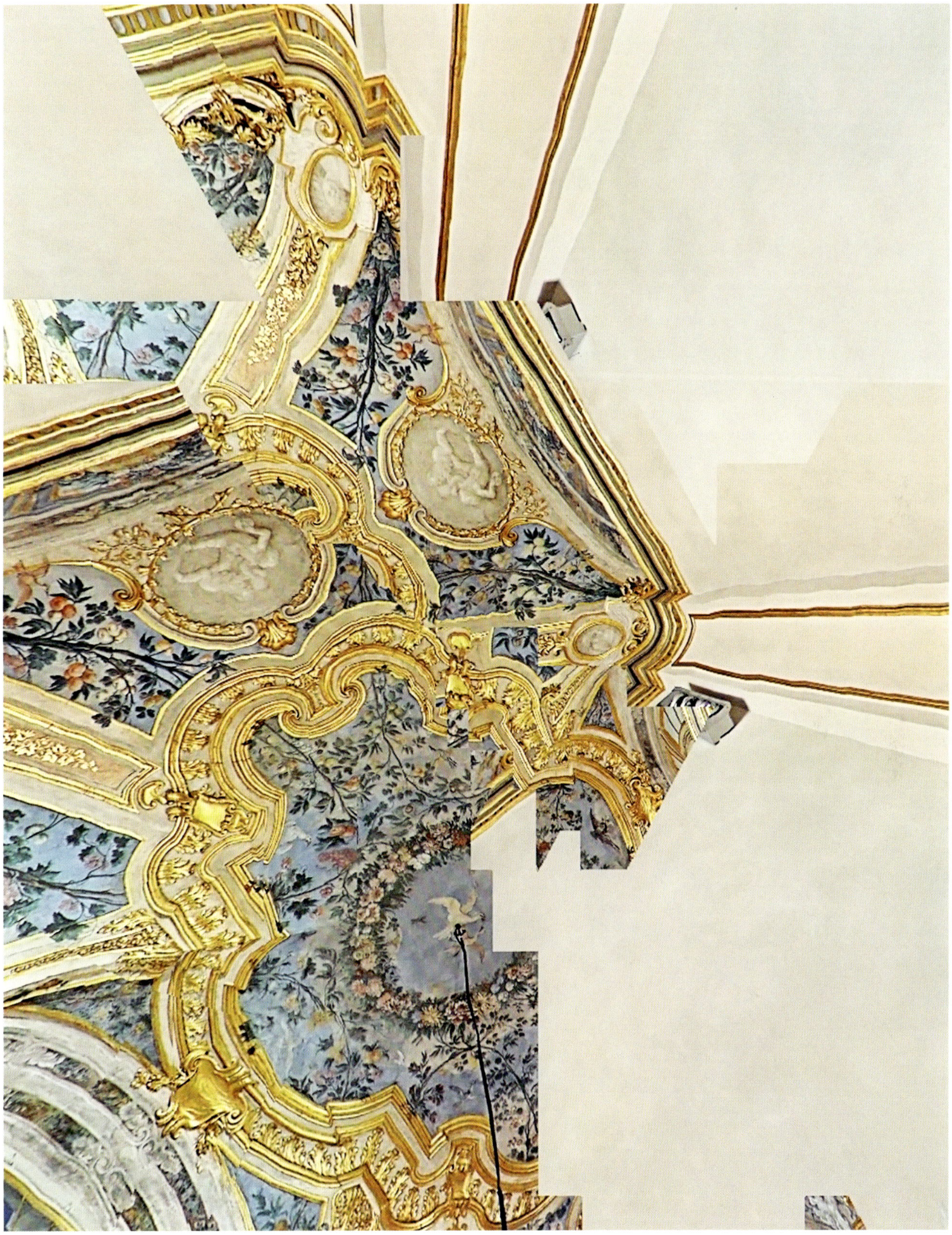

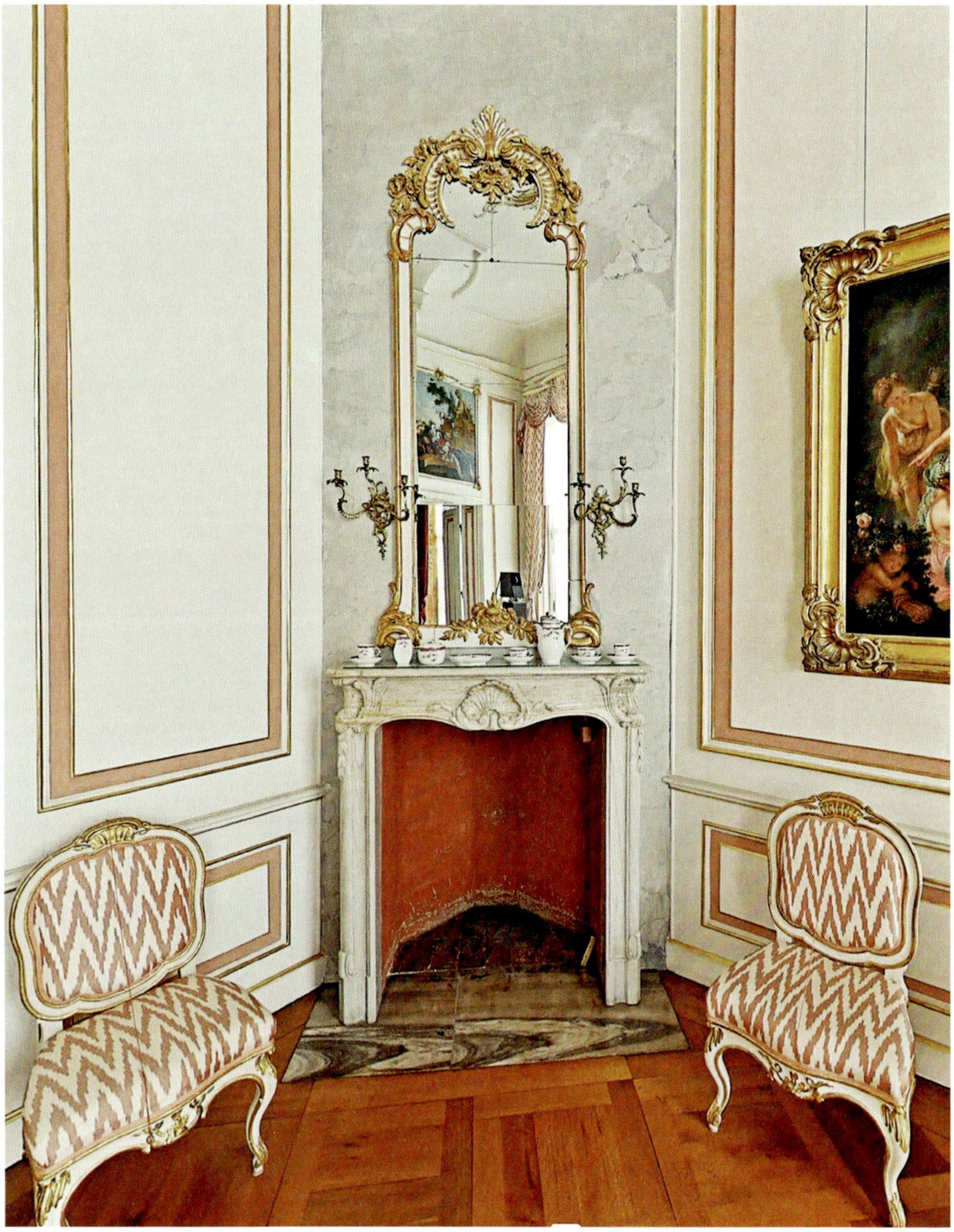

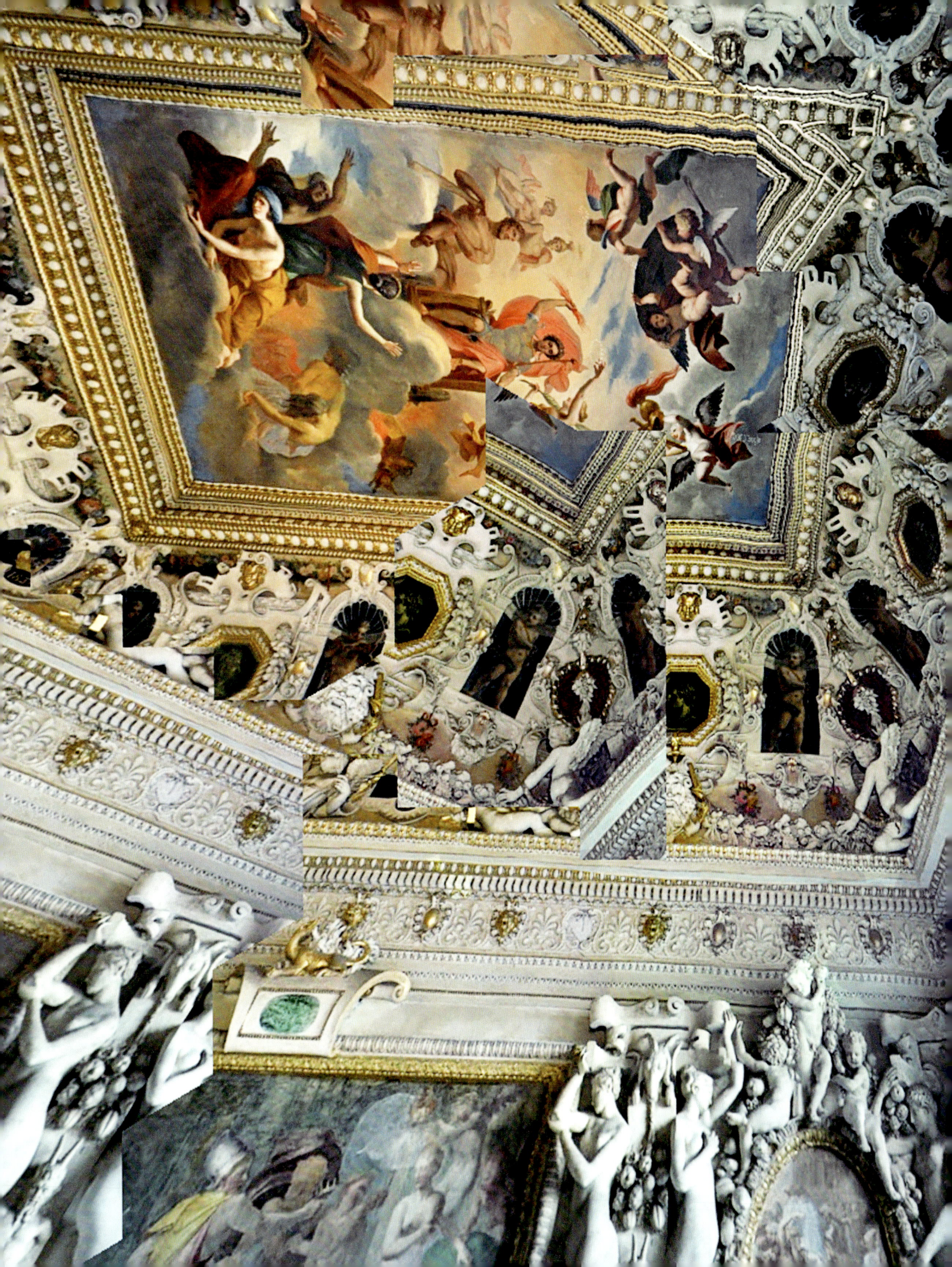

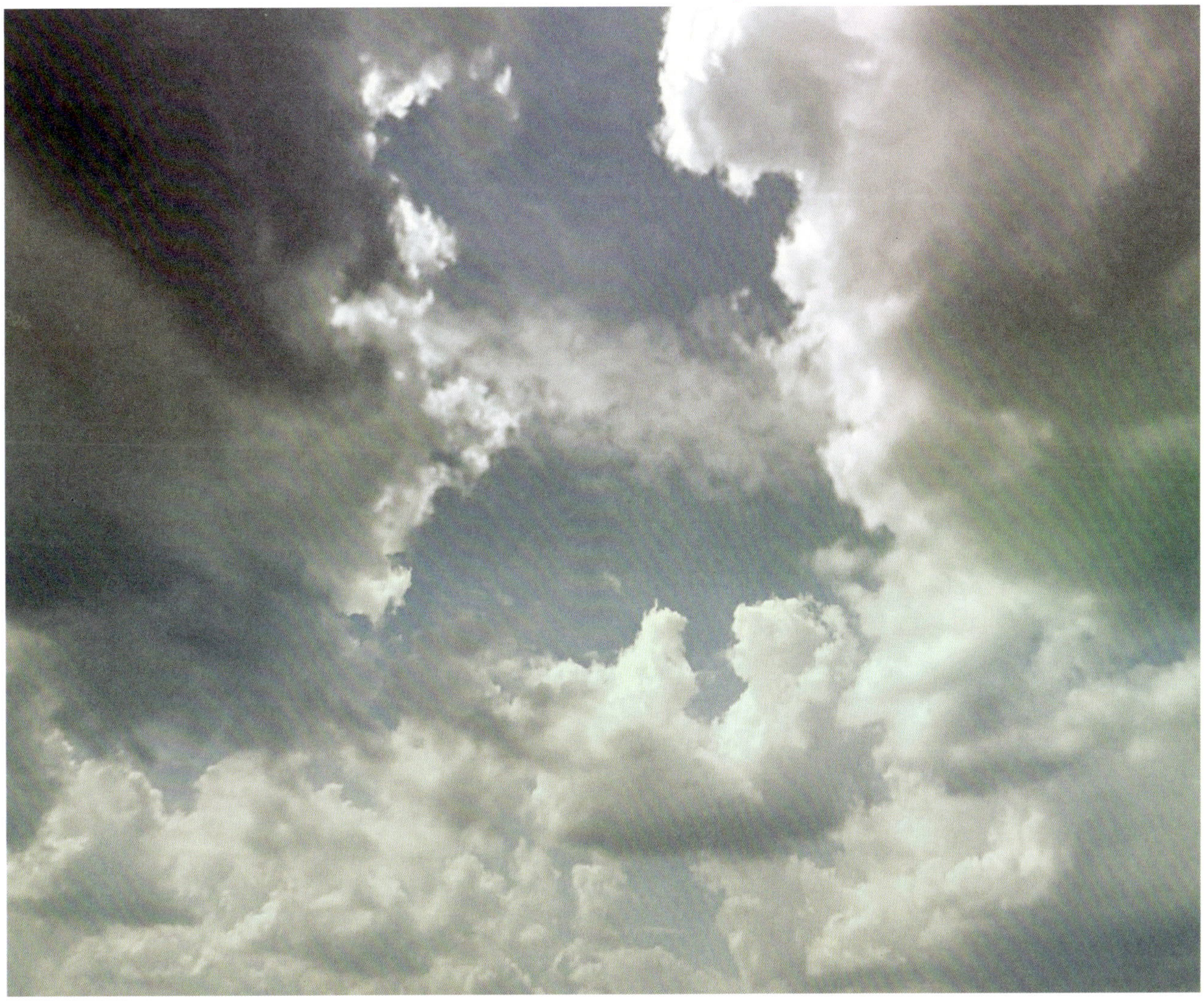

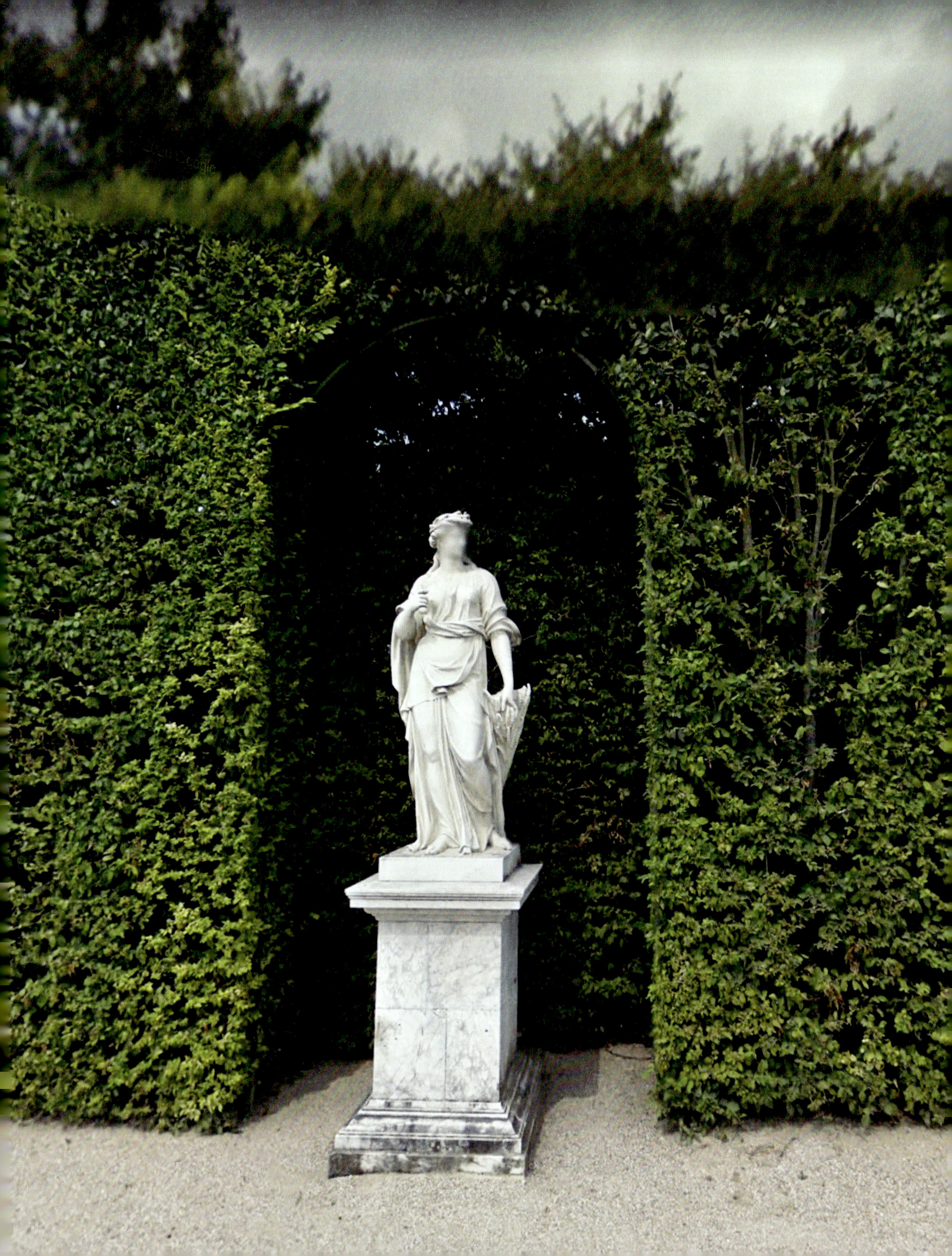

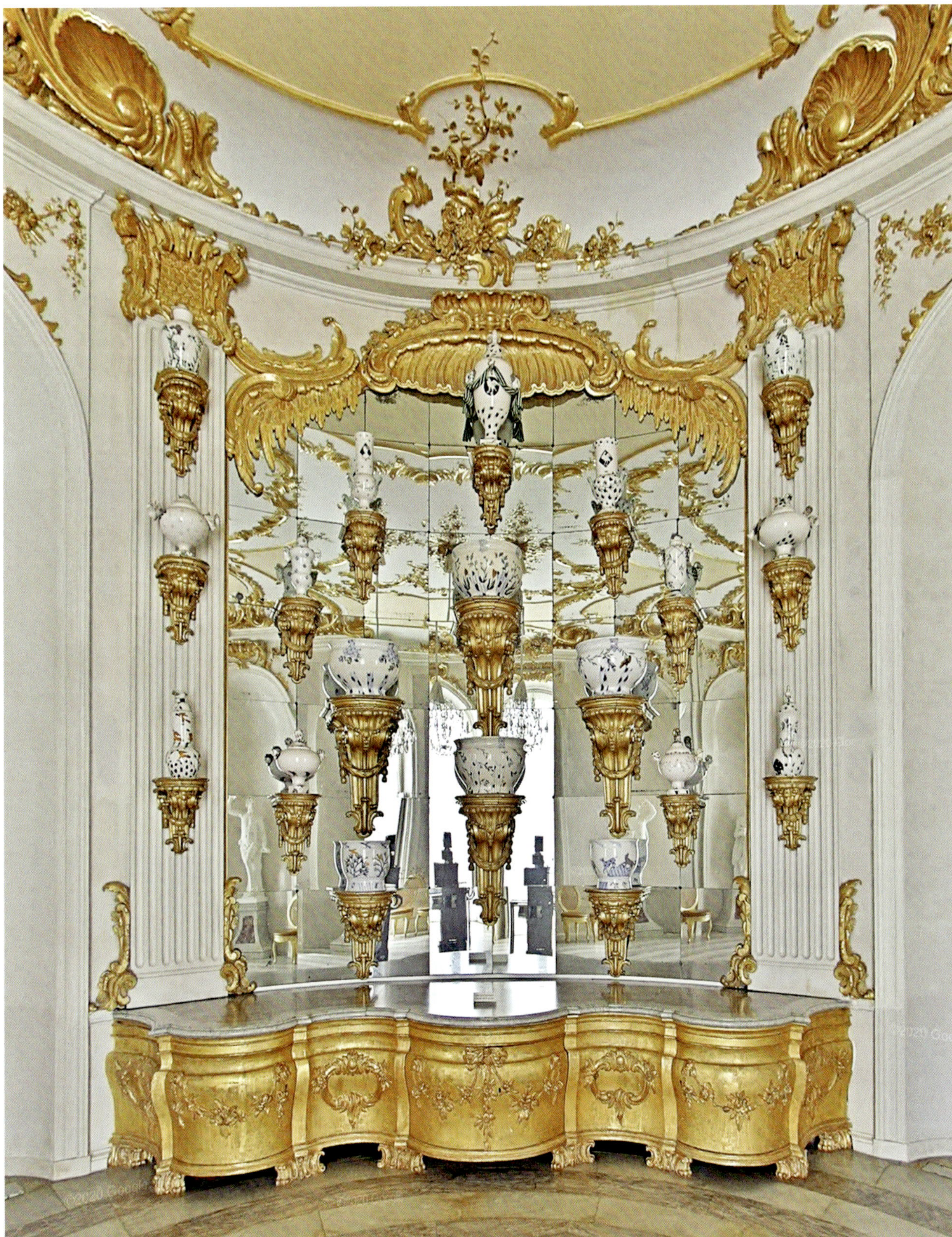

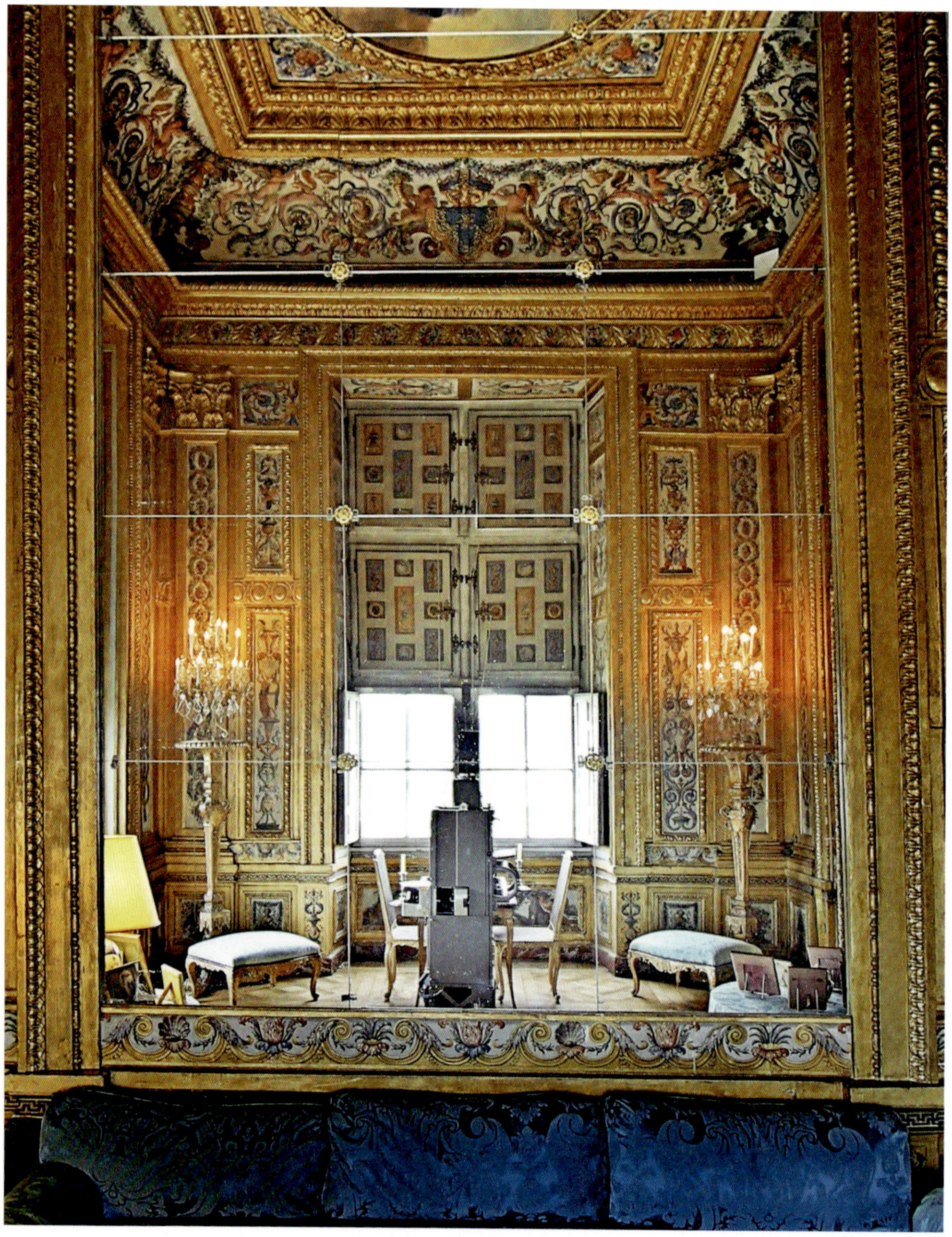

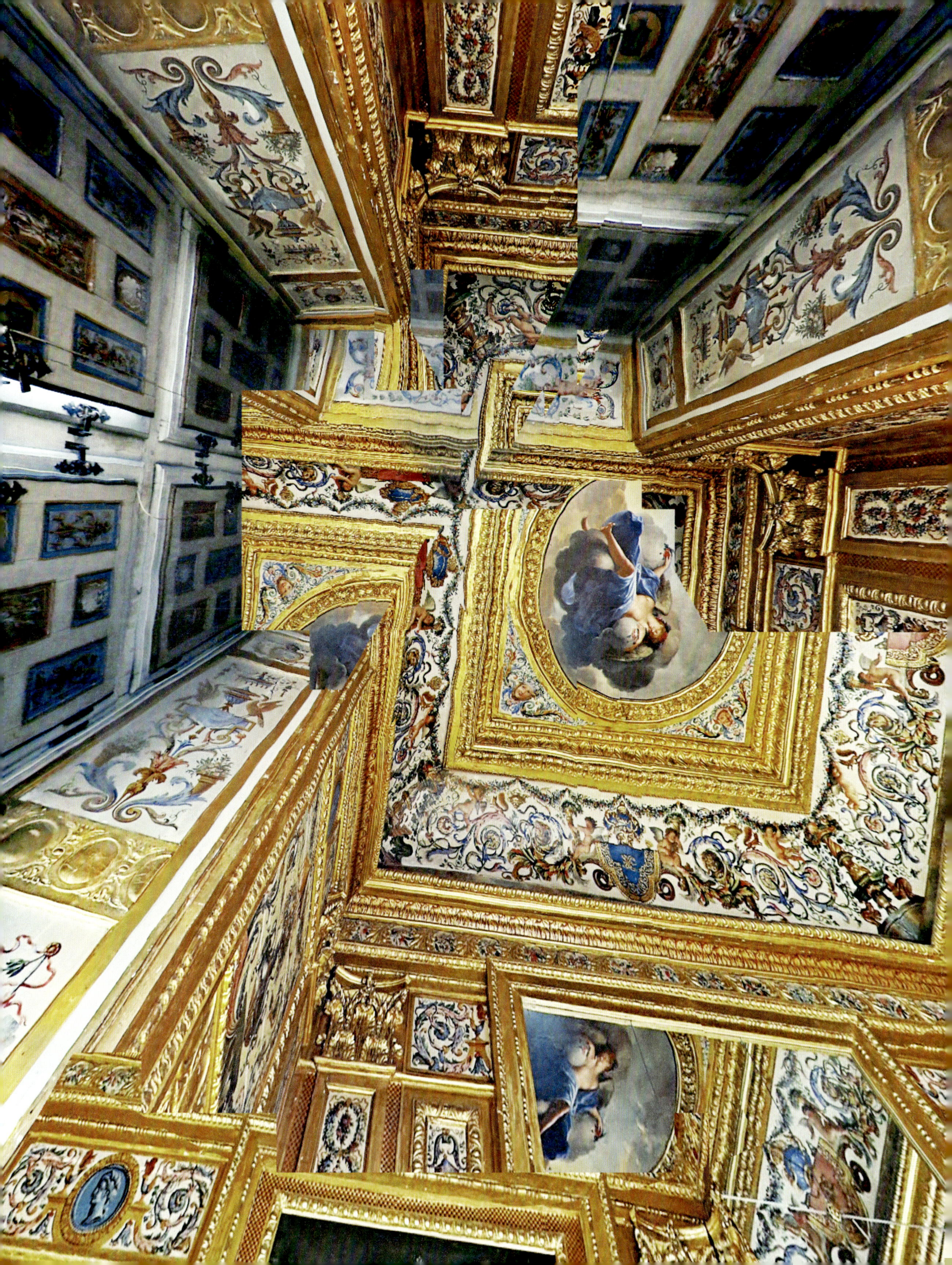

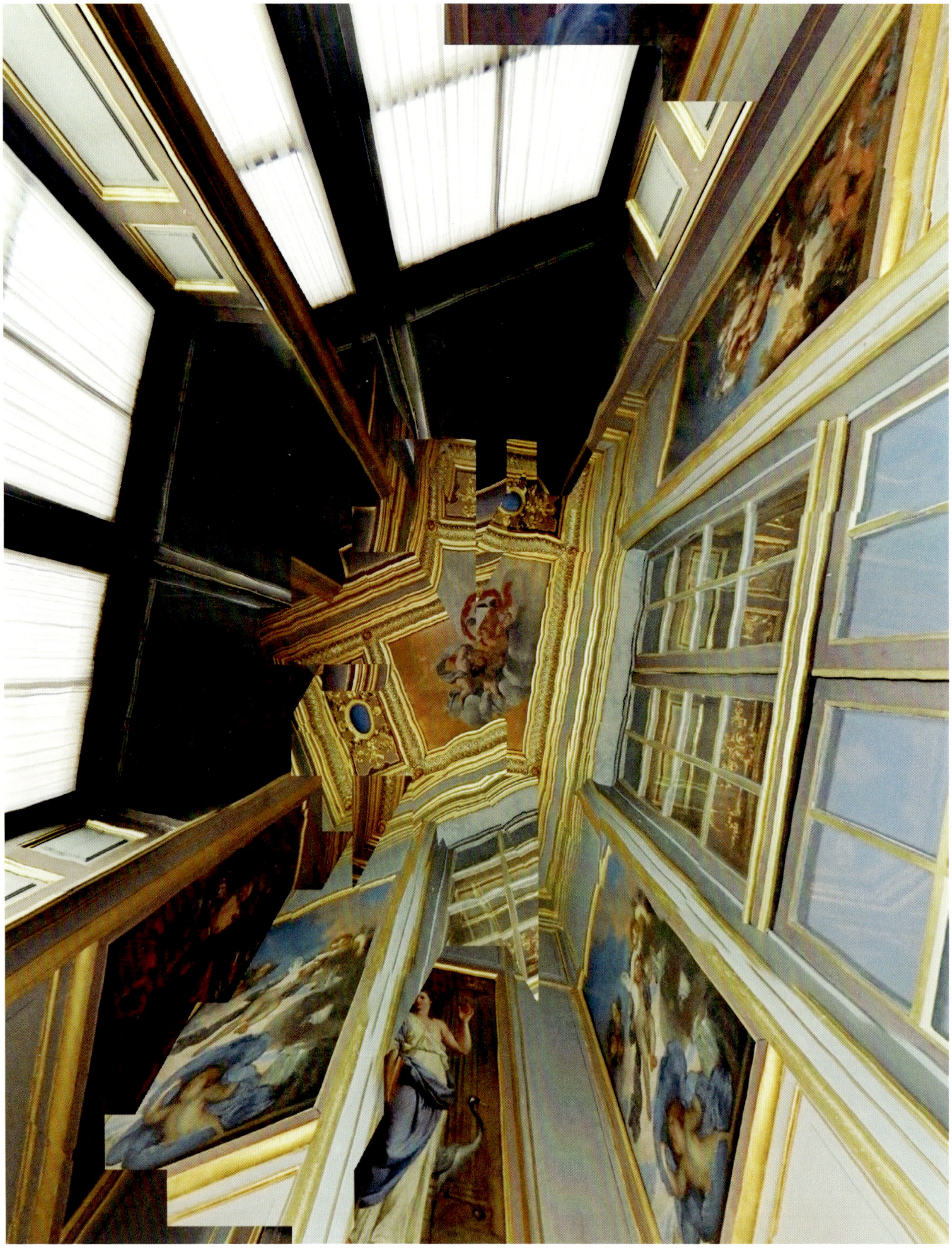

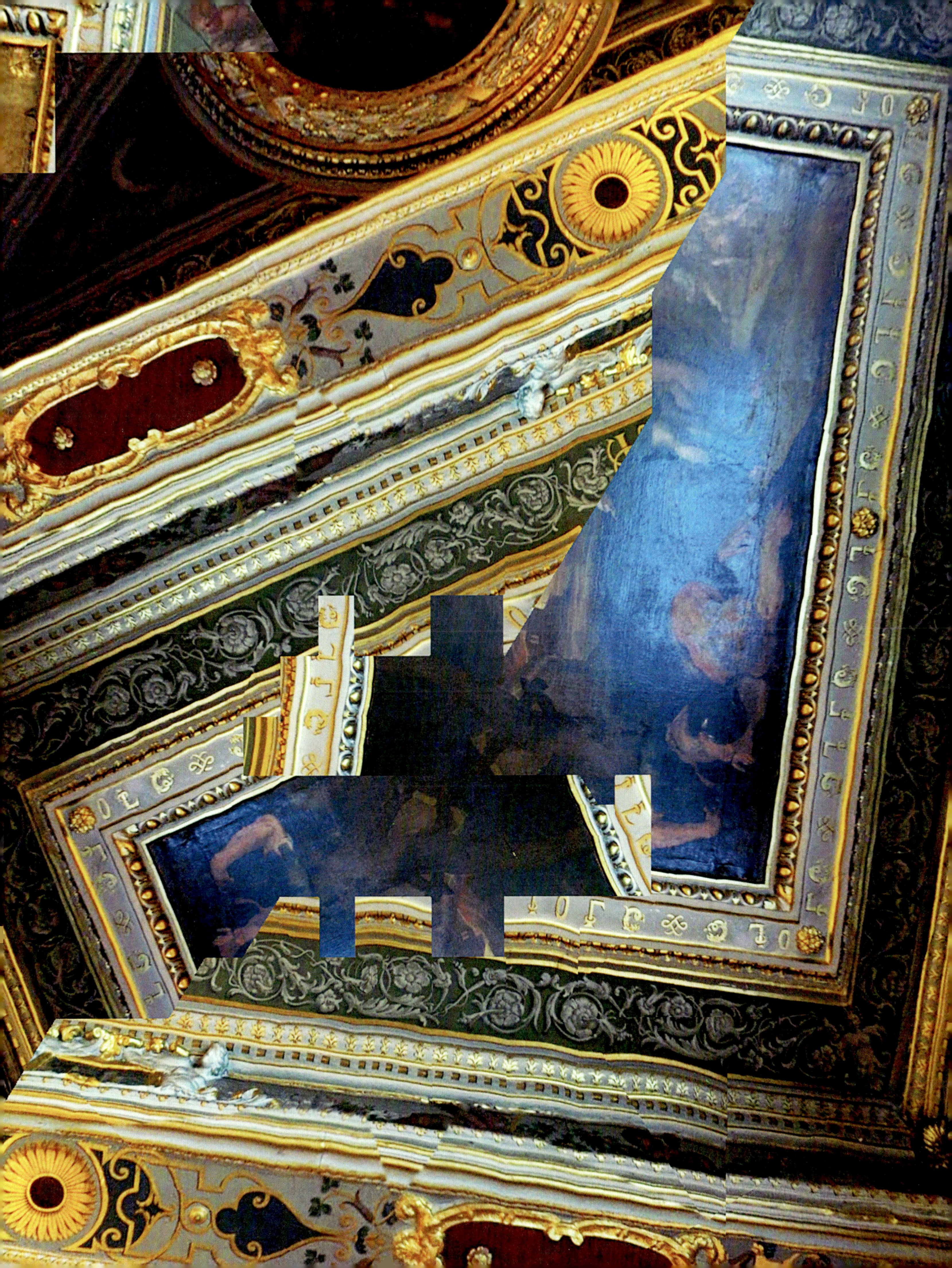

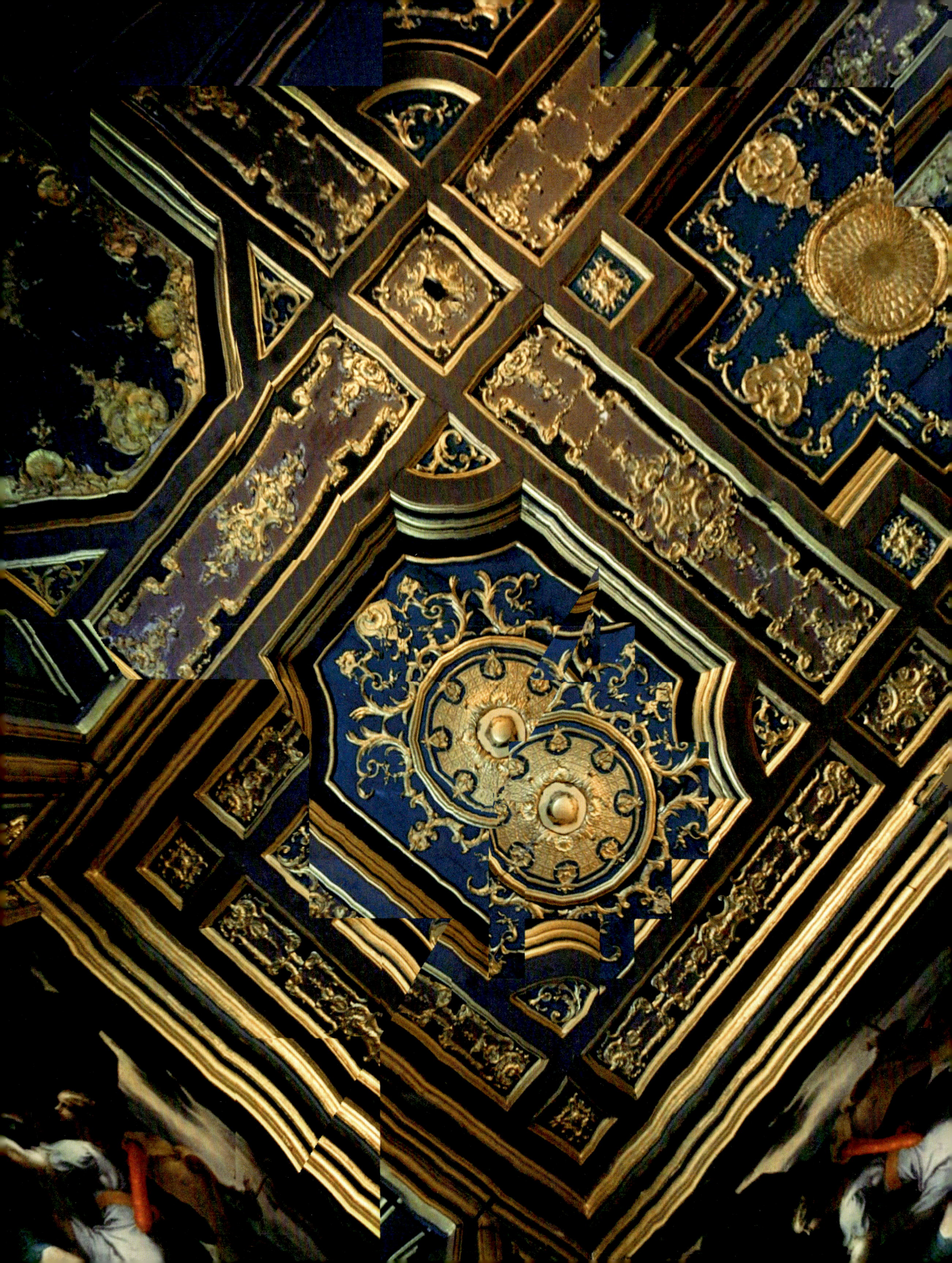

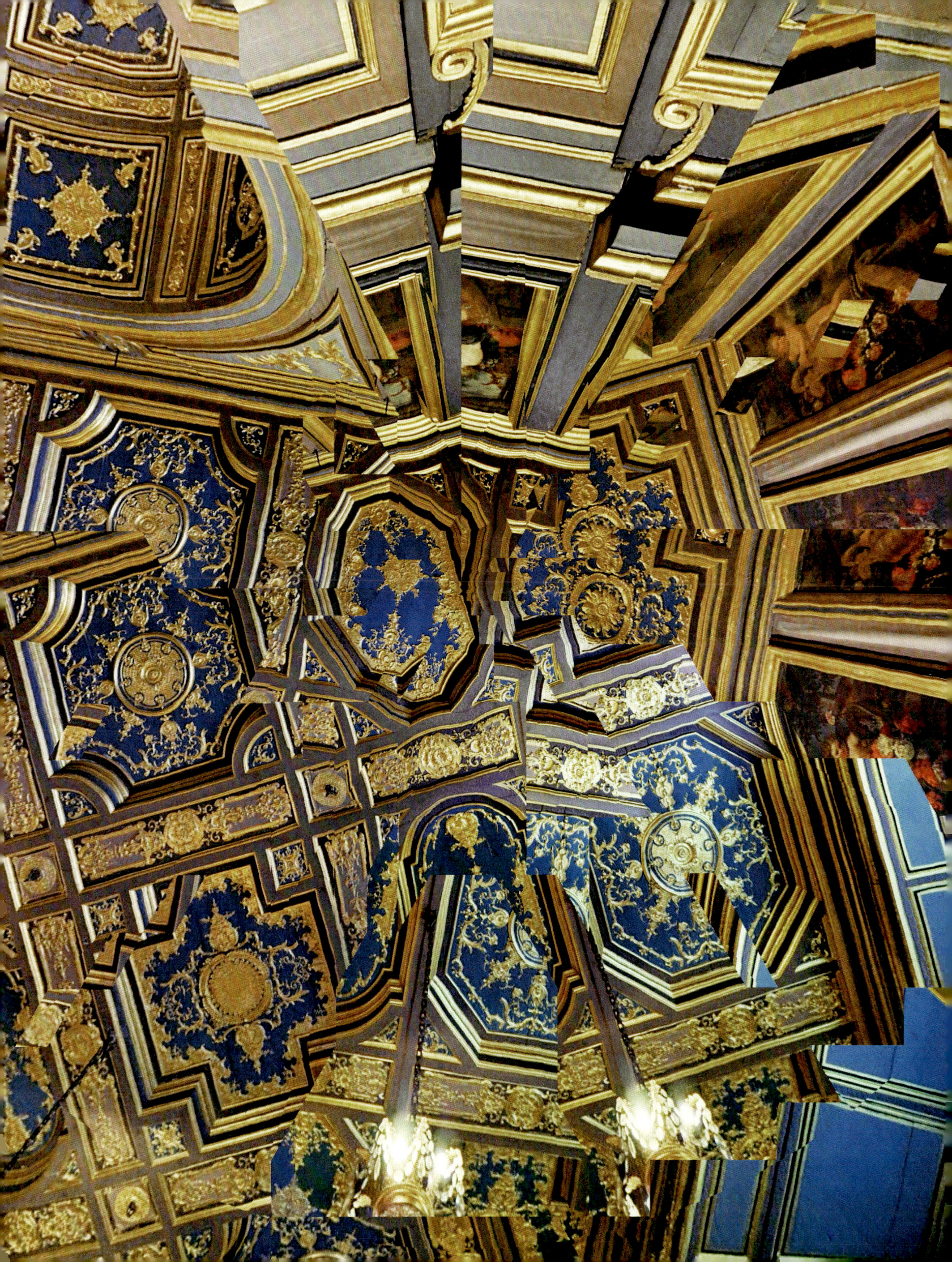

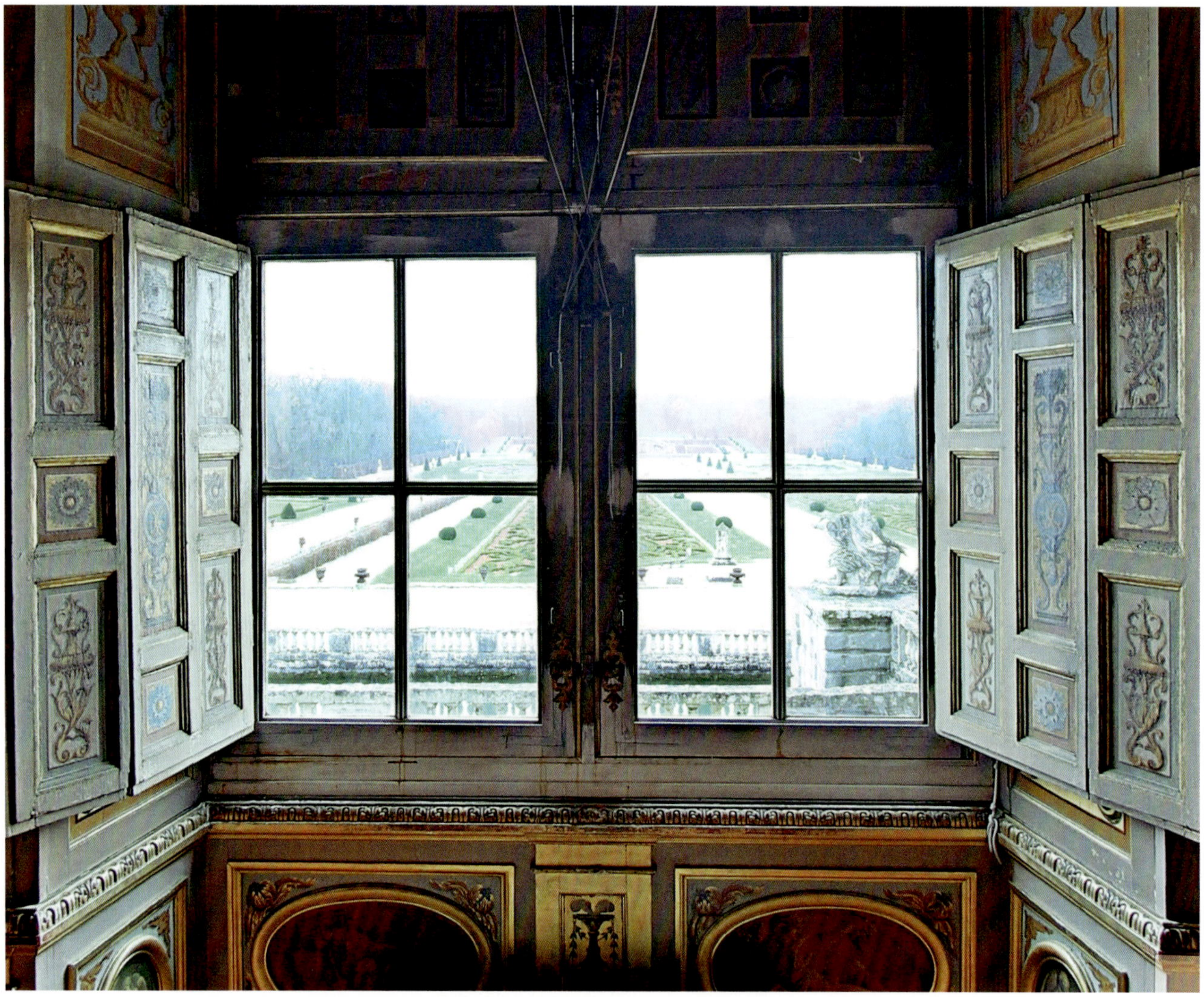

GRAND ILLUSION

Oh, the abhorrent spectacle of Baroque interiors, an affront to simplicity and a mockery of natural authenticity! This ostentatious display of opulence and excess, like a poisonous vice, creeps insidiously through the heart of society [. . .] Within these gilded walls and lavishly adorned chambers, I see a society lost in the delusions of its own grandeur, blind to the true essence of human existence.
— Chat GPT Jean-Jacques Rousseau, *Critique of Baroque Interiors*

In 2015, Theresa Ganz began taking screenshots during online forays into the Baroque palaces of Europe using Museum Views, a feature of the Google Cultural Institute. Souvenirs of the artist's virtual wanderings through the halls and grounds of chateaus and palazzos, the pictures presented here in book form are at once familiar and not quite of this world.

Museum Views, much like Google's widely adopted Street View, allows users to click through photogrammetric 3D models of illustrious locales from the convenience of their screens. Unlike an embodied museum visit, intended to engage many of the five senses, the virtual experience is by comparison constrained and graceless—one does not stroll so much as zoom to fixed points, from which to peer at 360-degree panoramas distorted by wide-angle lenses. The virtual tool, albeit absent of aura, offers tangible benefits. That these privileged spaces are now available for anyone to meander through—at any time, for as long as they wish, with no fee, no crowds, and ample (though unflattering) light—is a marvel of contemporary technology and diplomacy.

For Ganz, a second-generation American descended from World War II refugees, the coffered ceilings in the Château de Fontainebleau, dazzling ornamentation of the Palazzo Madama, and manicured gardens of Versailles inspired meditations about the role of art and artisanship in the articulation of power. At the same time, her curi- betrayed its seams: a robotic eye recording its own mirror image, an indiscriminate blurring of greenery and statuary faces. Patchwork collages unwittingly produced by glitches in Google's image-stitching program were the most uncanny instances of slippage. Acting as a proverbial ghost in the machine, Ganz recorded these flaws—even inducing them, to Cubist effect, until software updates prevented it.

On one level, Ganz's catalog of aberrations serves as a critique of Baroque and Rococo decadence, whimsically deconstructing an aesthetics of awe commissioned by regimes whose extravagant tastes were underwritten by colonialist exploitation and suppression of the masses. Her screenshots subvert the imposing ornamentation of her subjects, rendering it fatuous and absurd. In this she aligns with Jean-Jacques Rousseau, who railed against Baroque excess and correlated the flourishing of the arts with moral decline before developing a vision of society that guided the French Revolution—which in turn precipitated the transformation of these seats of empire into sites dedicated to fostering public appreciation of past glory.

BY JOSHUA CHUANG

The title *Grand Illusion*, a nod to Jean Renoir's classic 1937 film, poses the question of who is deluded and what artifice is being exposed. Set in the prison camps of World War I, *La Grande Illusion* centers on the relationship between a French captain, de Boëldieu, and his sympathetic German captor, von Rauffenstein. Both are aristocrats, and they find that they have a great deal more in common with each other than with their respective compatriots from the lower classes. Tragedy ensues when the two men are compelled by duty to perform as officers on opposing sides: de Boëldieu creates a distraction that allows his fellow prisoners to escape, and von Rauffenstein fires a fatal shot to stop him. "For a commoner, dying in a war is a tragedy," says de Boëldieu to a grief-stricken von Rauffenstein. "But for you and me, it's a good way out." In de Boëldieu's final moments, the two men lament that their nobility will become obsolete in the new world order.

Renoir's period piece, conceived as Adolf Hitler threatened to violate the Treaty of Versailles, offered insight into the myth of European civility and unity, a myth that was shattered by World War II yet still persists today. Ganz's screenshots—the majority taken during the Trump presidency—re-interrogate that myth as represented by the gaudy details and gold-encrusted surfaces of her subjects, recognizing them as a source of modern décor now notoriously referred to as "dictator style."

If the myth of the nation-state was central to the aspirations, anxieties, and brutality of the twentieth century, central to our present hopes and fears is the anodyne promise of technology. In revealing wrinkles and fissures in the simulacrum, Ganz points to a new illusion, one whose implications have yet to play out. Amid widespread praise for Google's efforts to break down barriers of access to great works of art and culture, nearly inaudible is the drumbeat of skeptics who have warned against the seductions of corporate altruism. Google's offer to convert symbols of monarchical power into usable assets presents a solution of convenience for these bastions of tradition, which risk becoming irrelevant in a world where one does not exist if one can't be found online. This apparent act of goodwill is also undoubtedly a form of welfare capitalism where access to—and ultimately dominion over—information is not really free or unbiased, but rather part of an encompassing, long-term strategy cunningly developed to extract profit and exert influence, where narratives of art and history continue to be shaped by the preferences and priorities of the few.

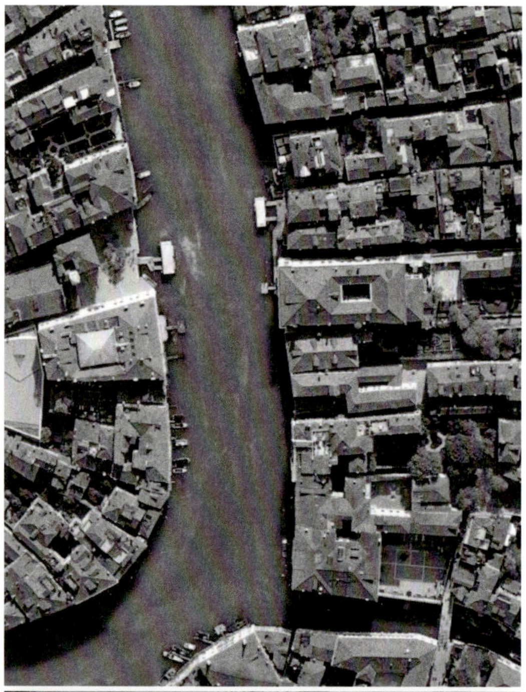

Ca'Rezzonico,
Venice, Italy

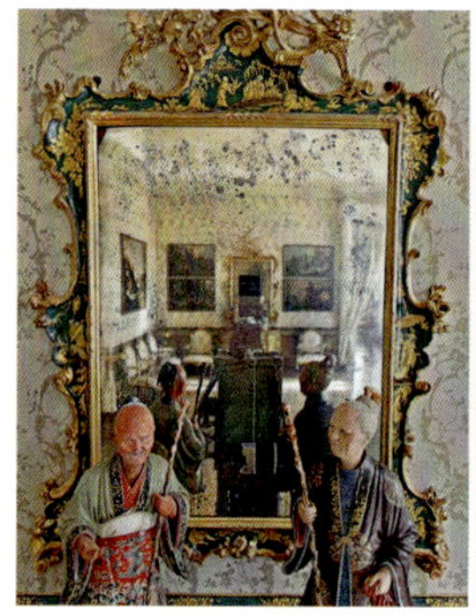

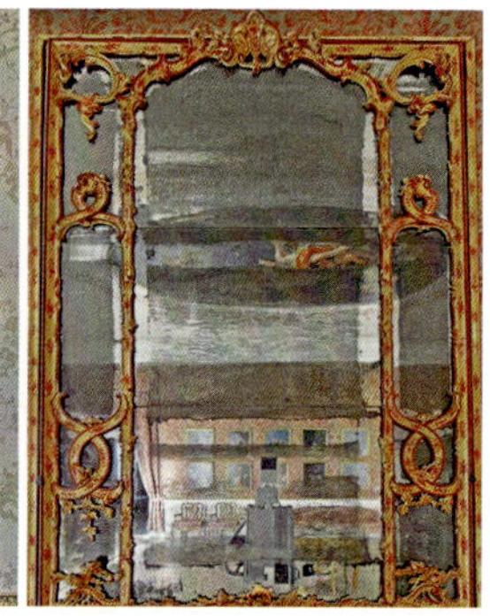

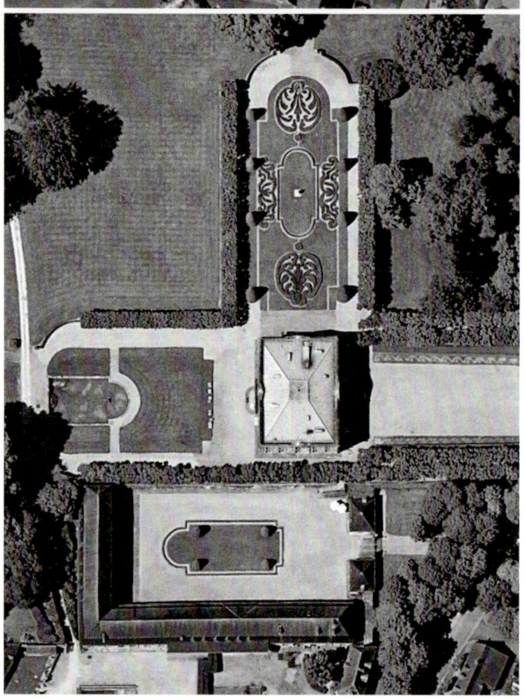

Château de Bouges,
Bouges-le-Château, France

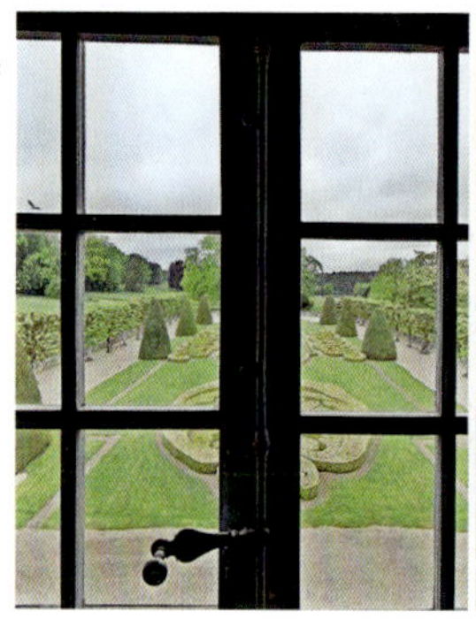

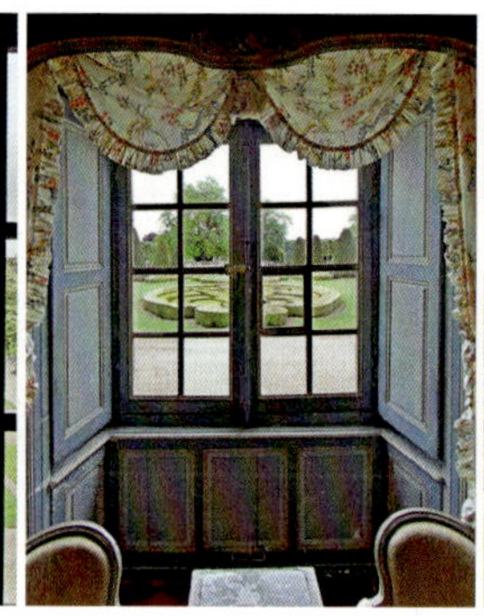

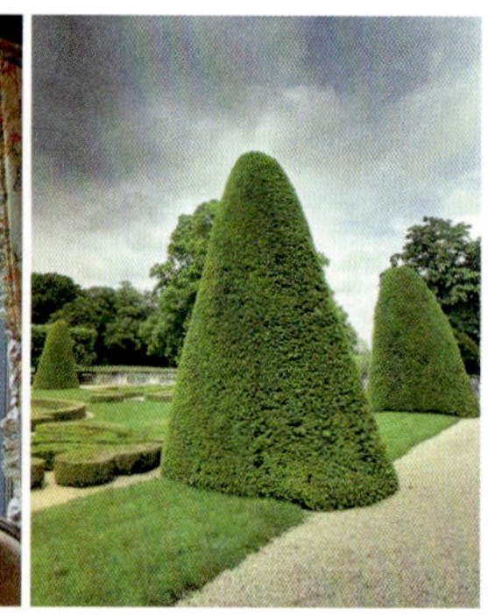

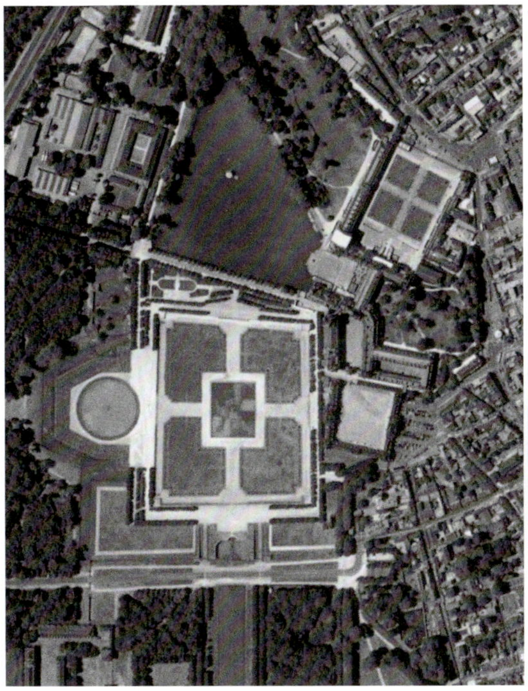

Château de Fontainebleau,
Fontainebleau, France

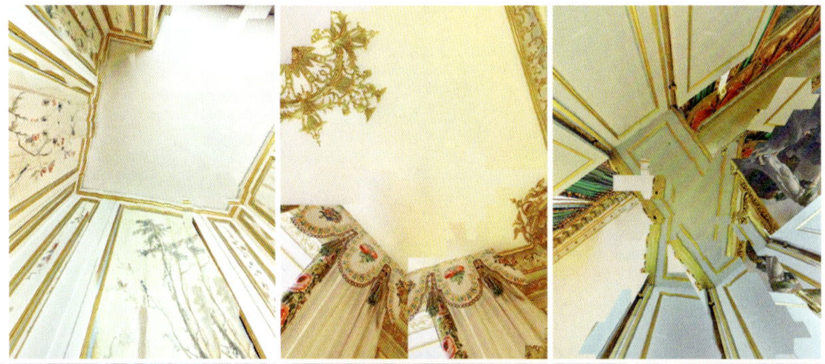

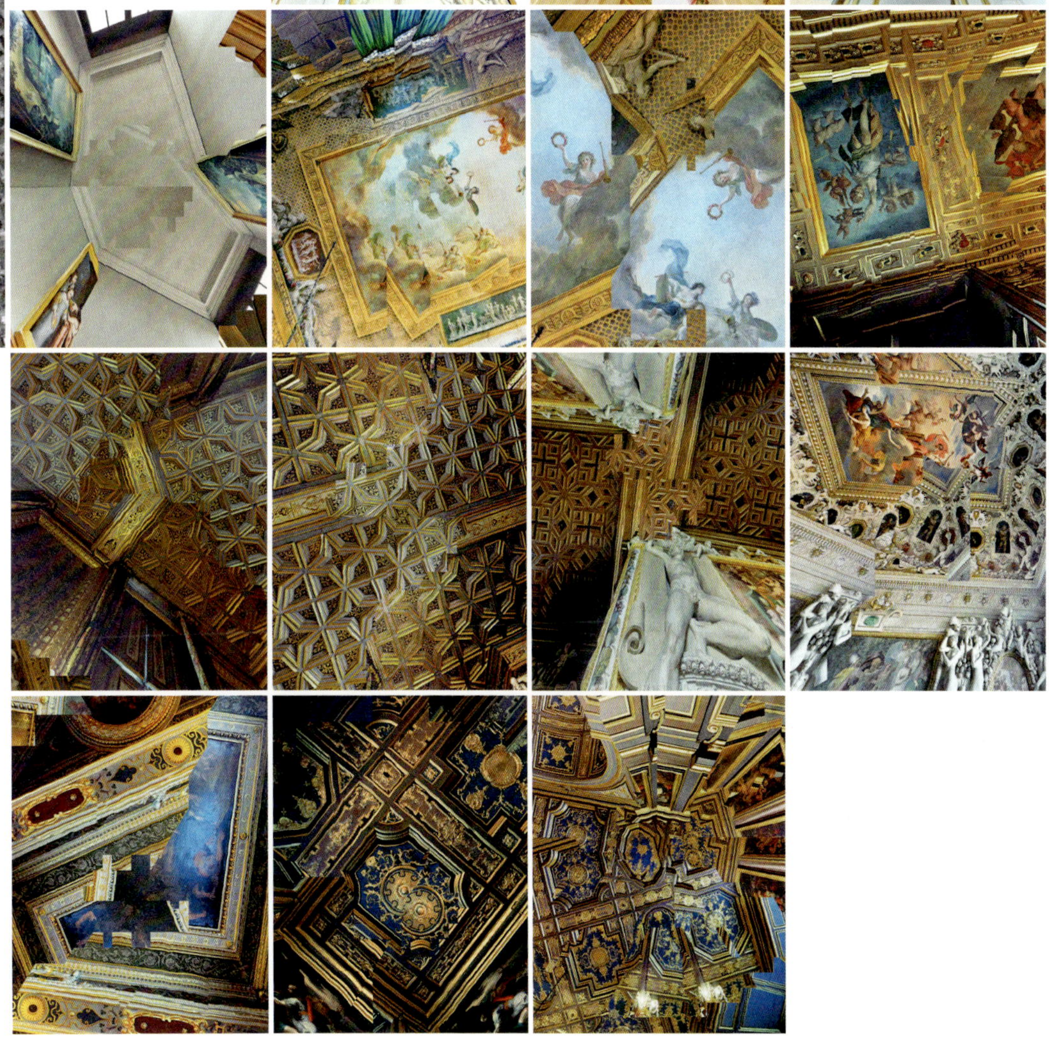

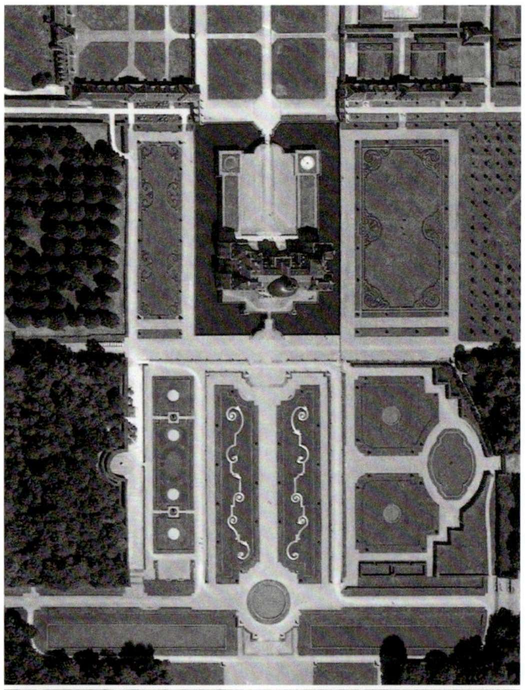

Château de Vaux-le-Vicomte,
Maincy, France

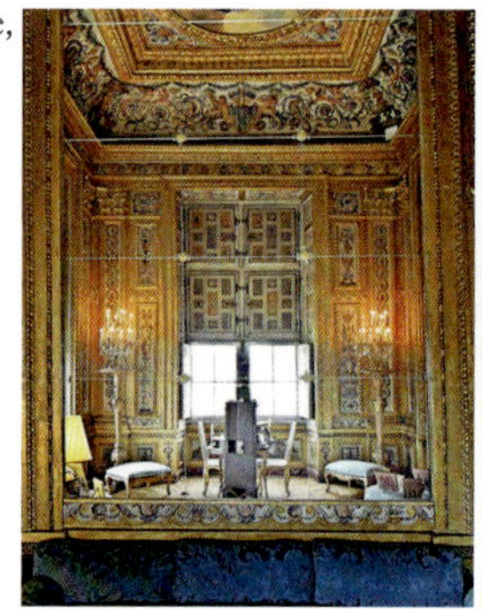
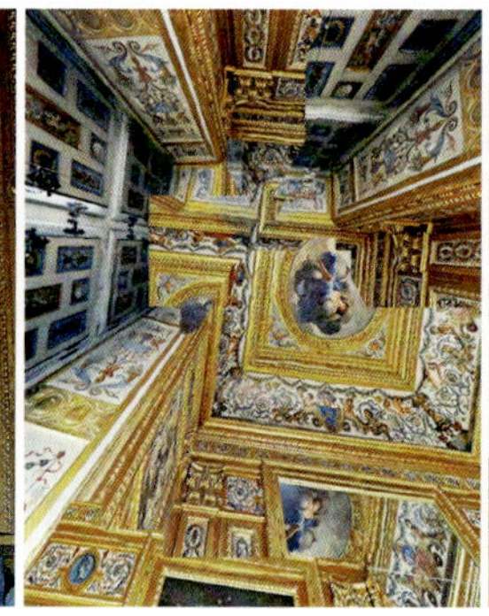
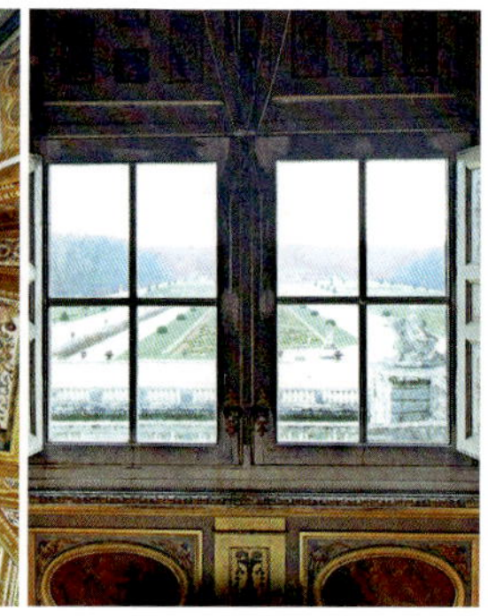
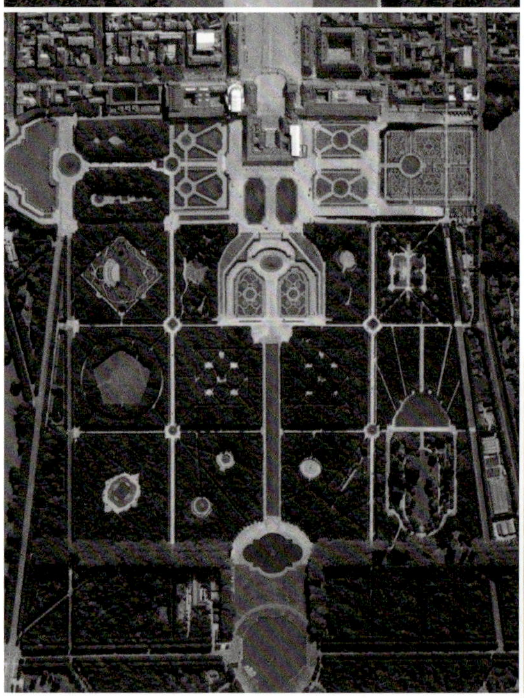

Château de Versailles,
Versailles, France

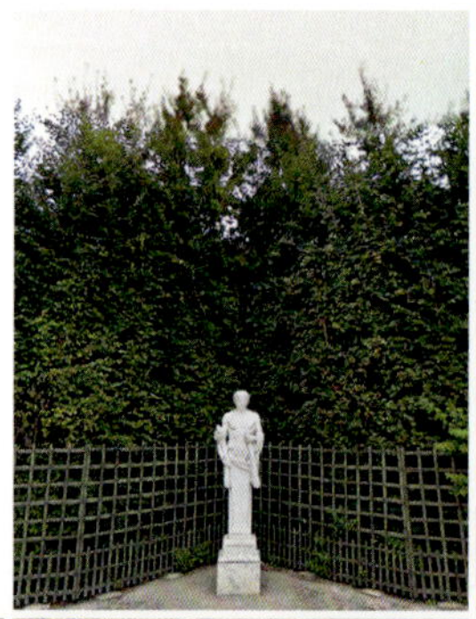
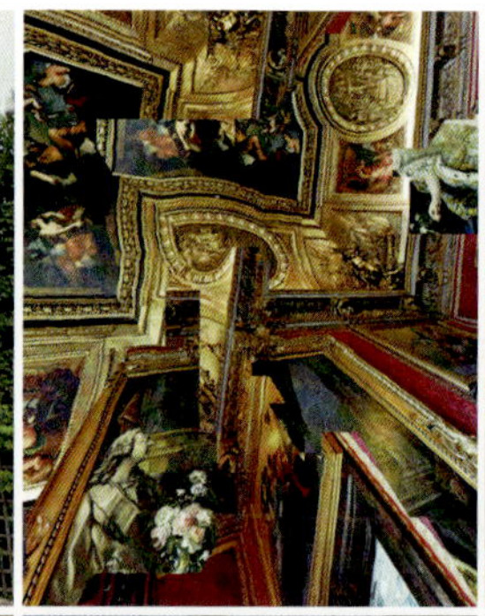
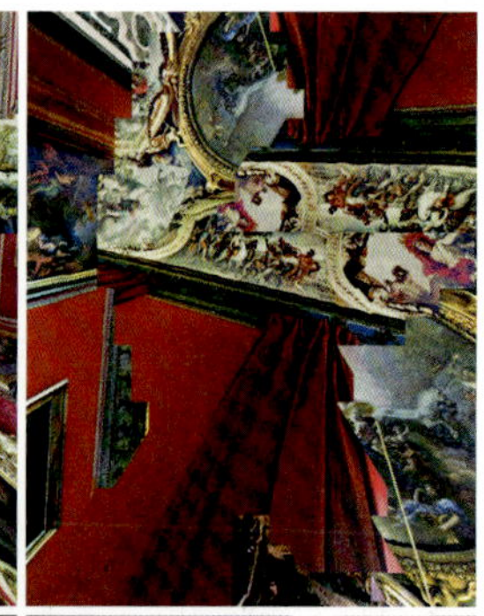
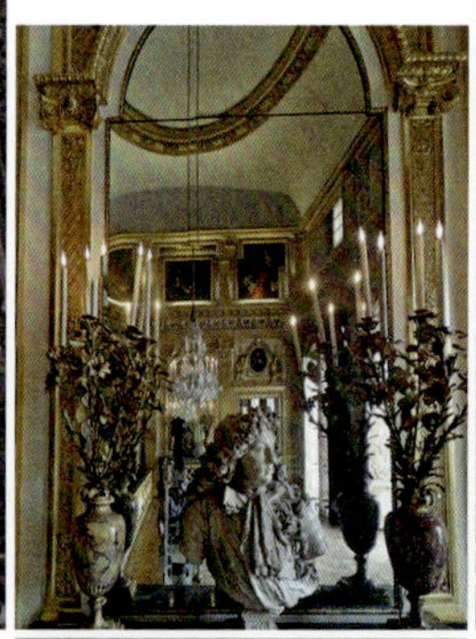
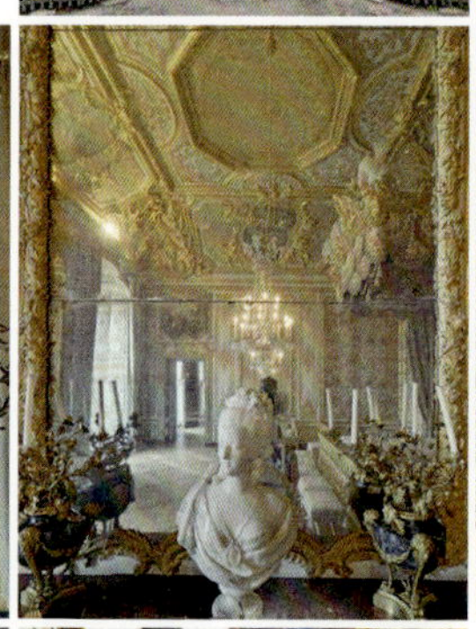
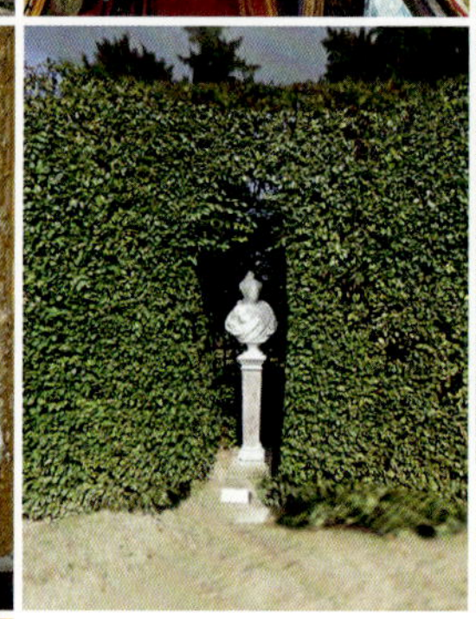
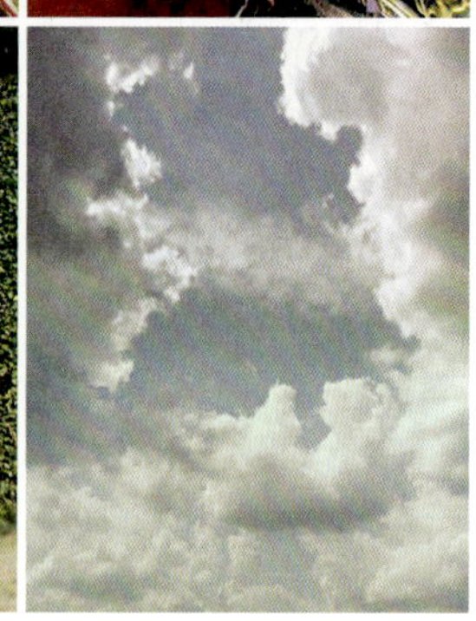
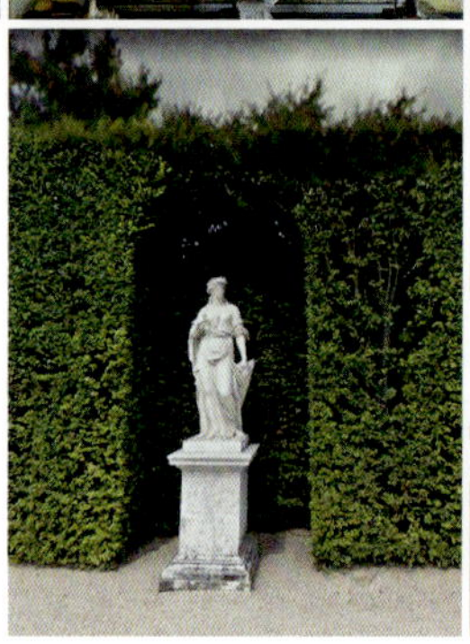
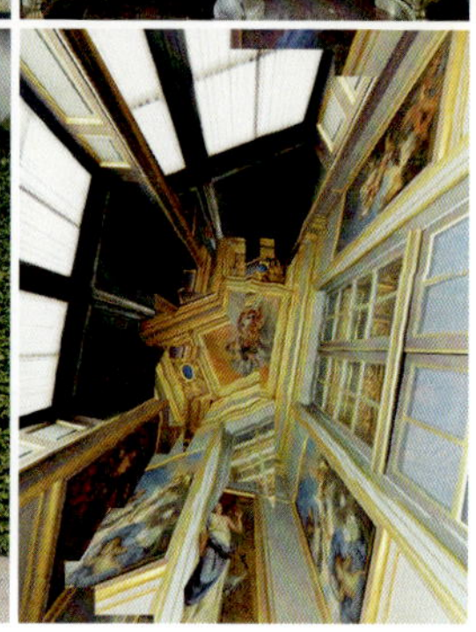

Jardins du Luxembourg,
Paris, France

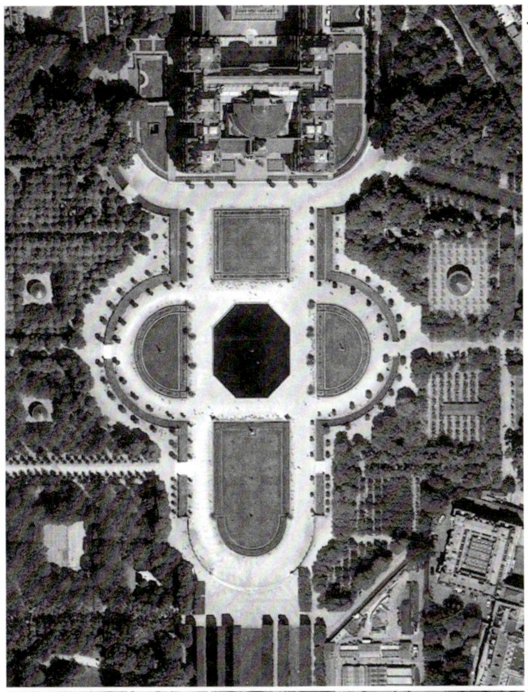

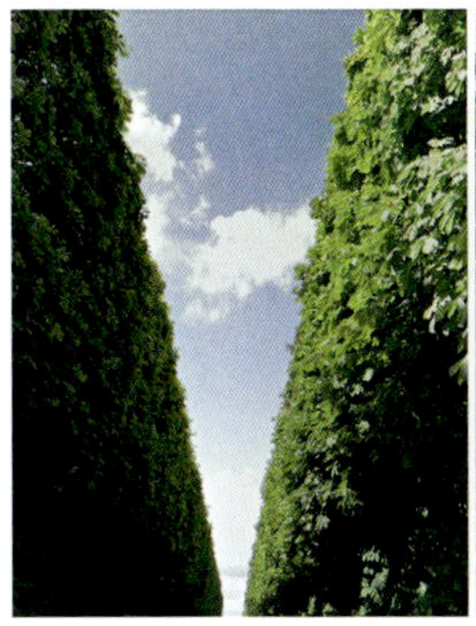

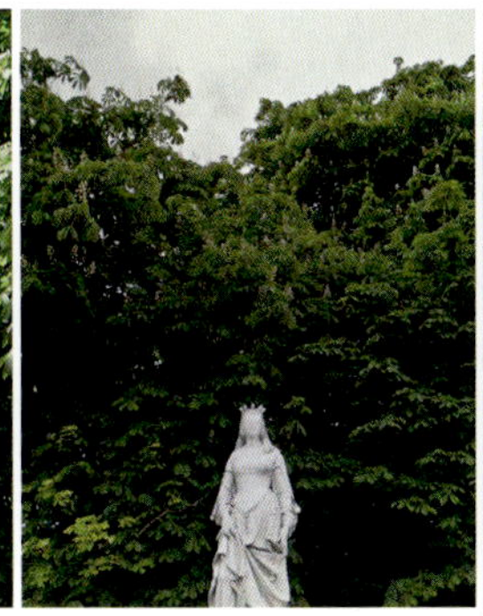

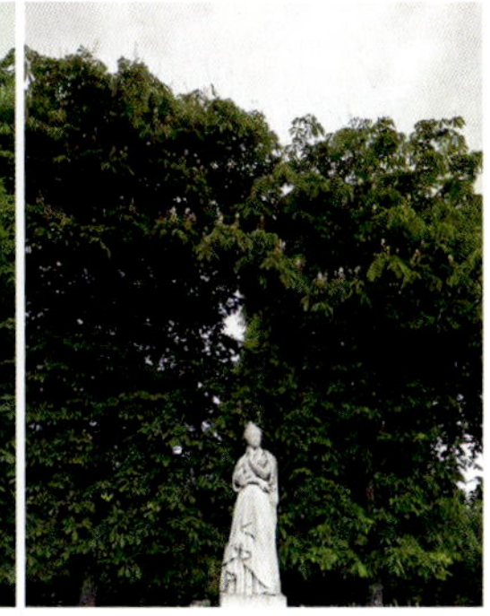

Palácio Nacional de Queluz,
Queluz, Portugal

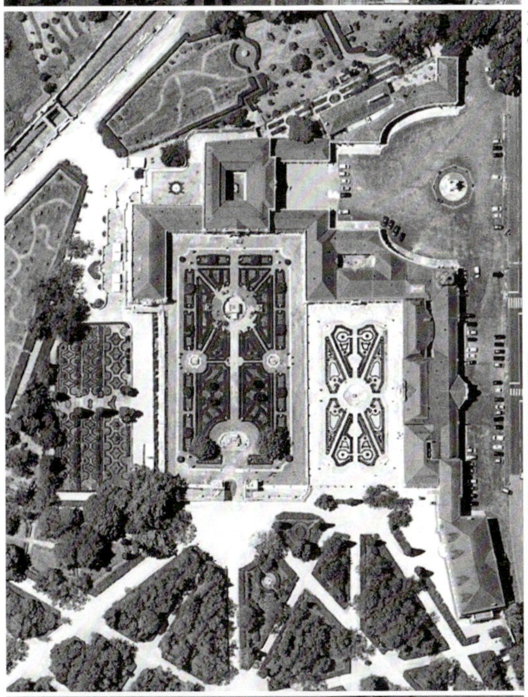

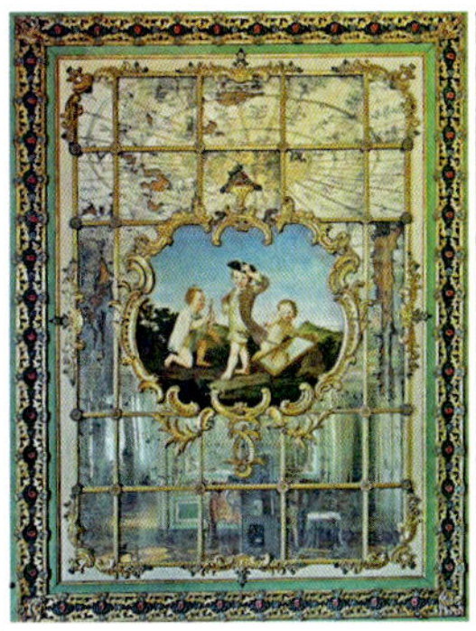

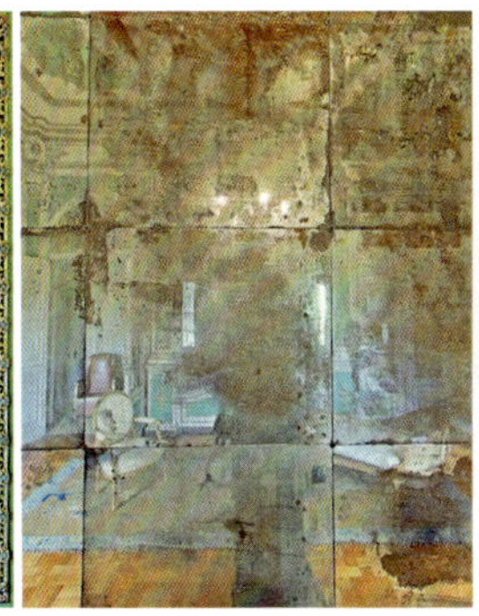

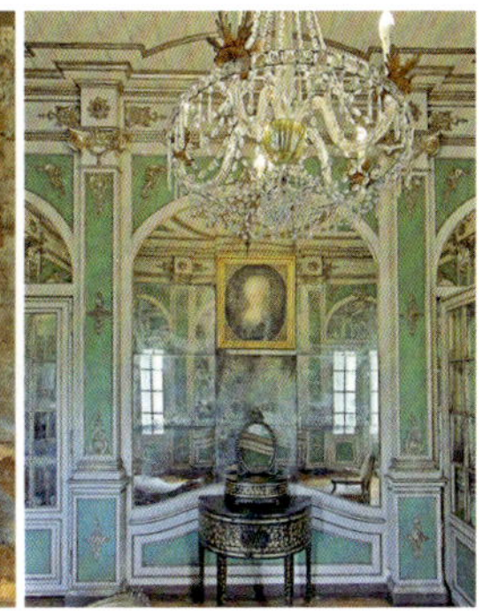

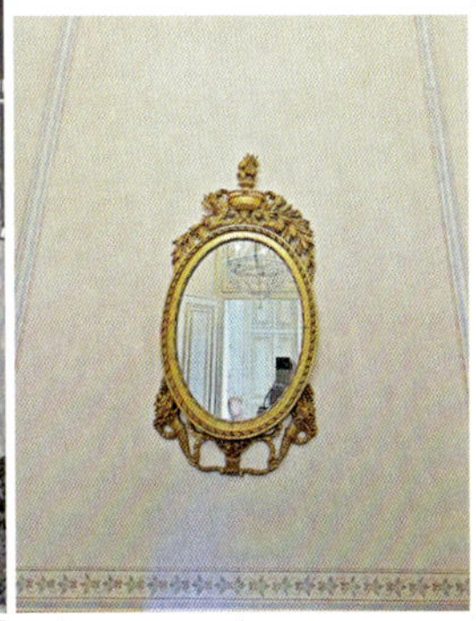

Palazzo Ducale,
Venice, Italy

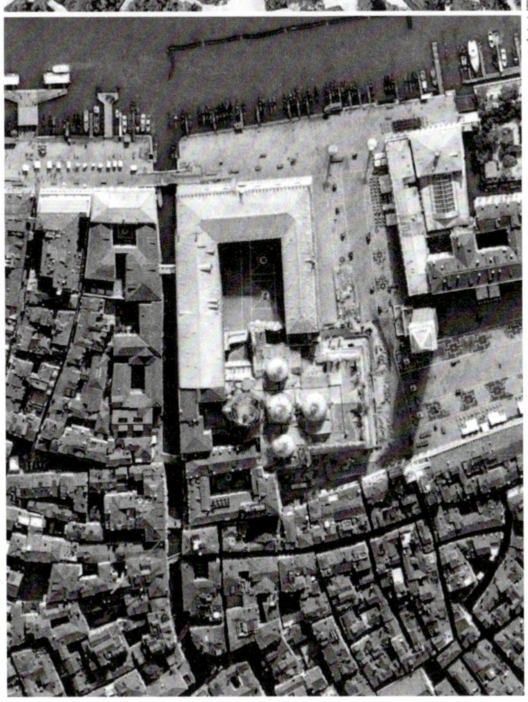

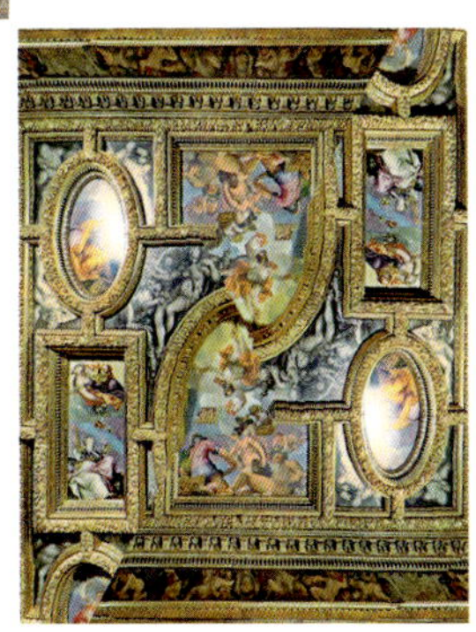

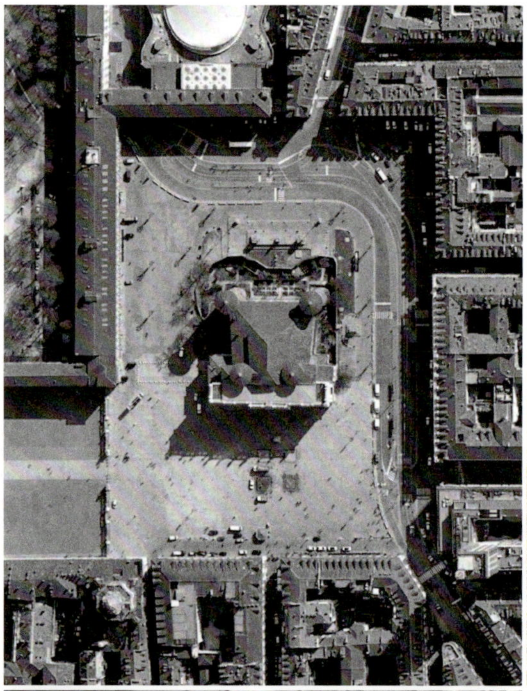

Palazzo Madama,
Turin, Italy

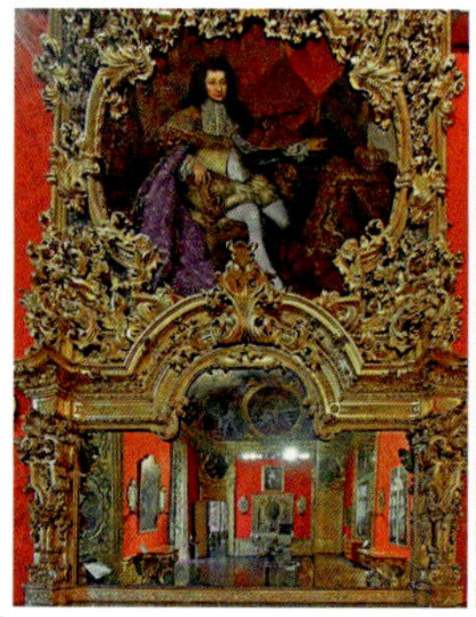

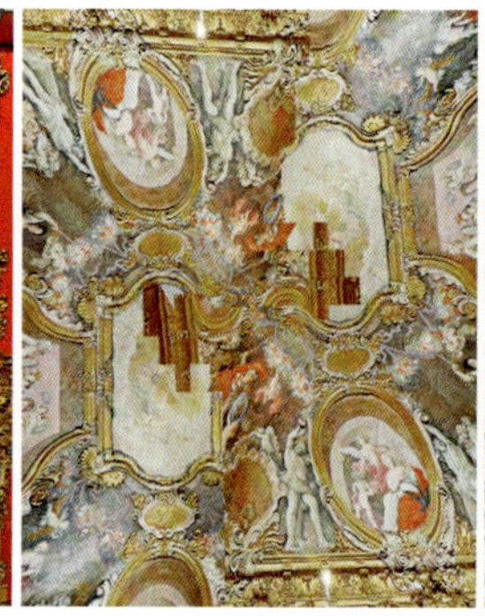

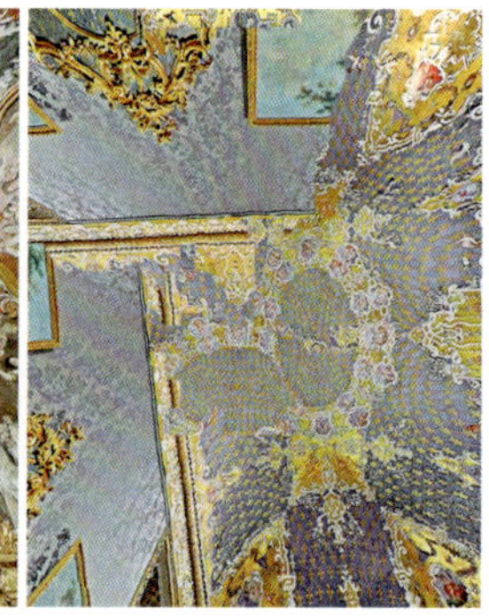

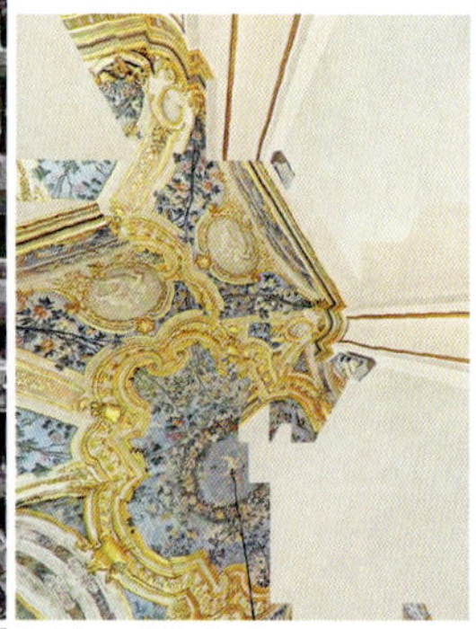

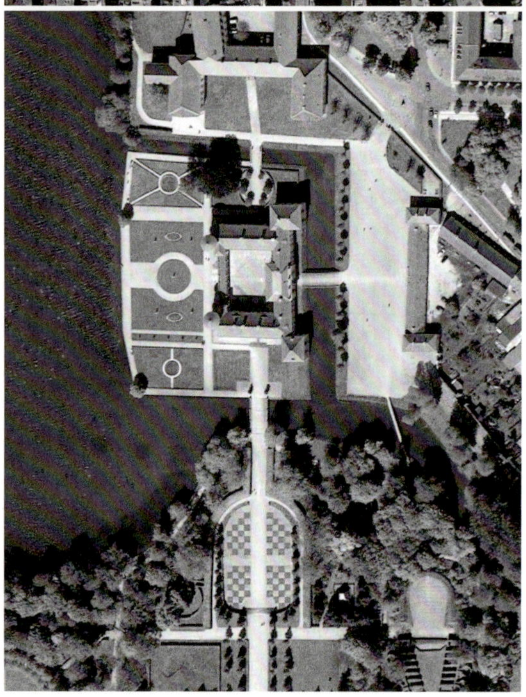

Schloss Rheinsberg,
Berlin, Germany

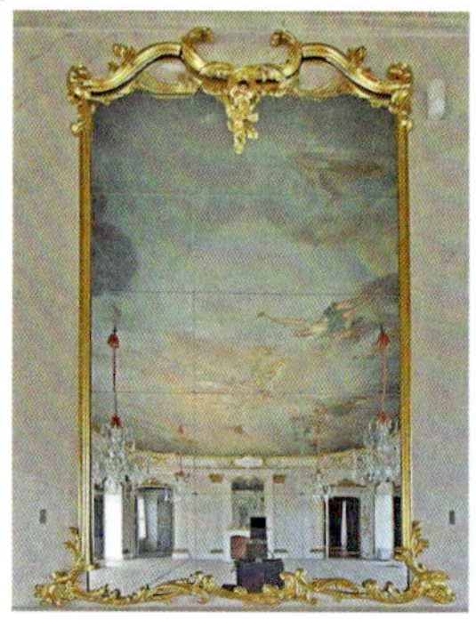

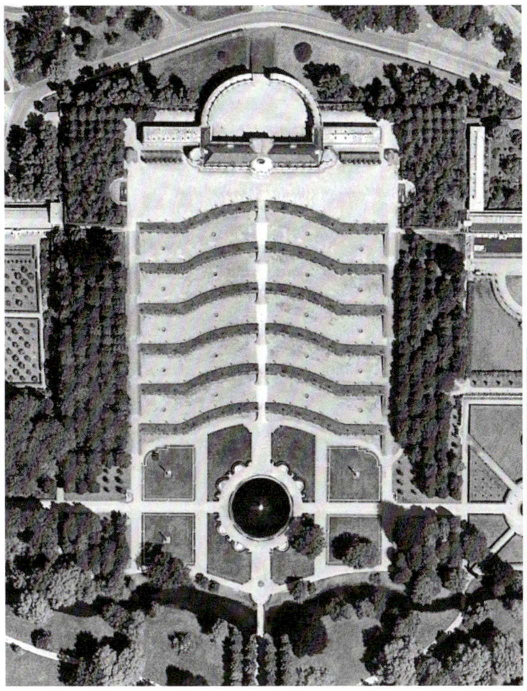

Schloss Sanssouci,
Potsdam, Germany

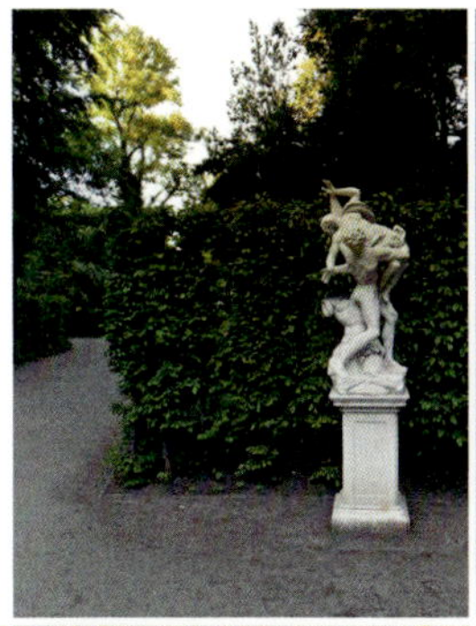

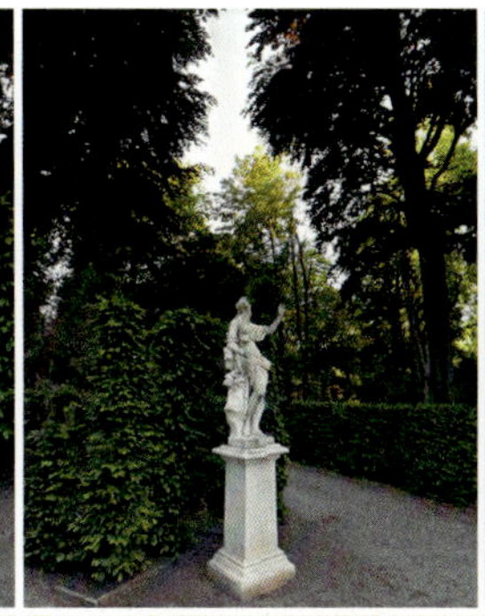

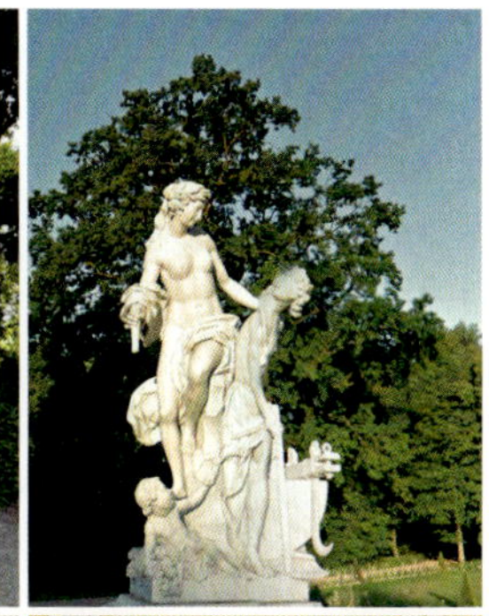

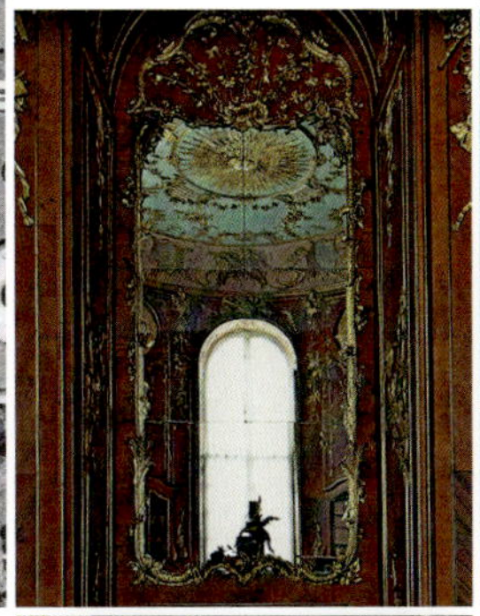

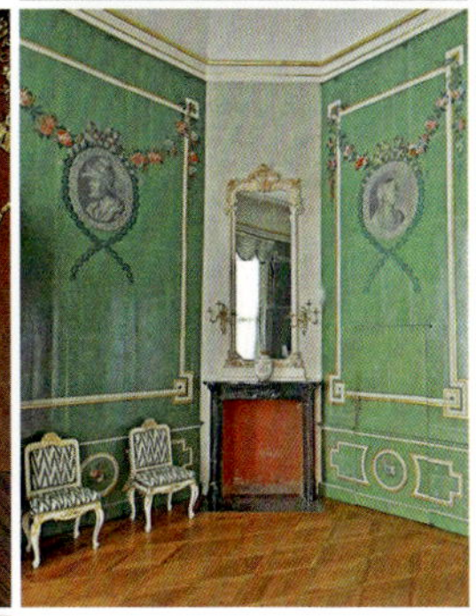

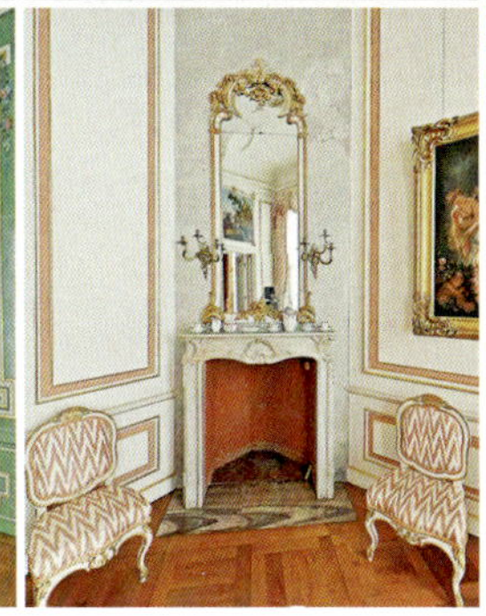

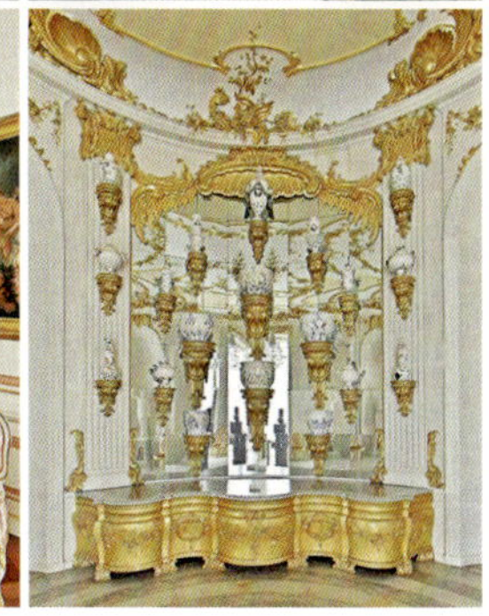

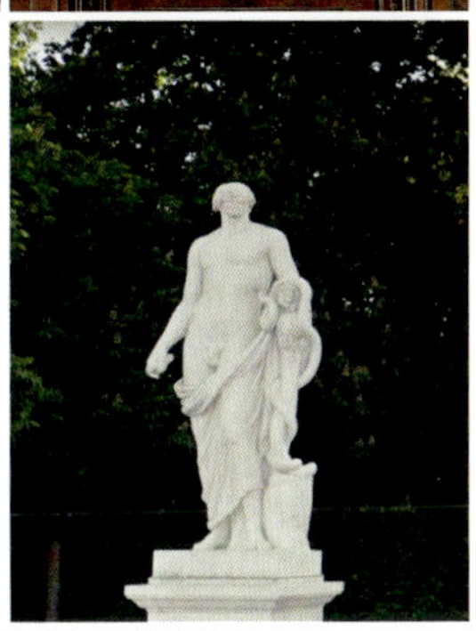

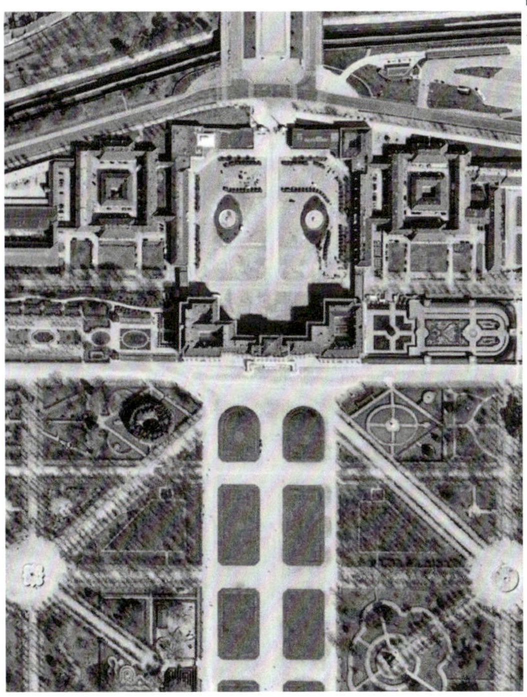

Schloss Schönbrunn,
Wien, Austria

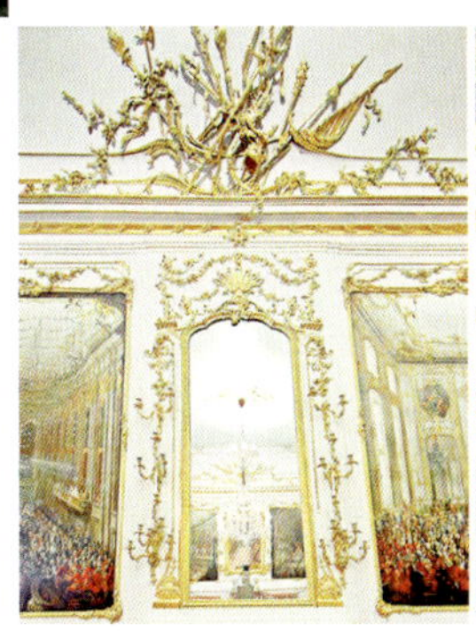

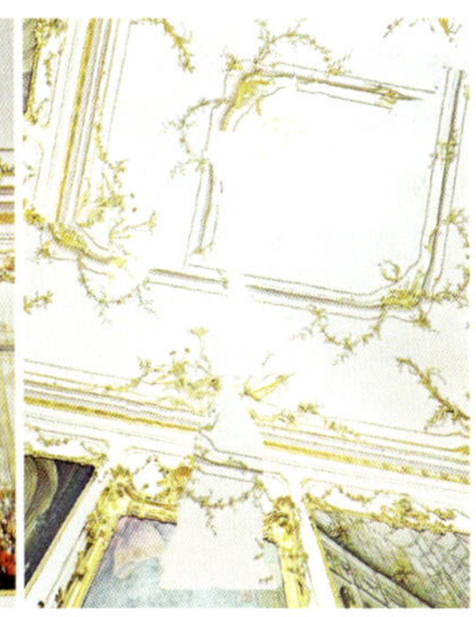

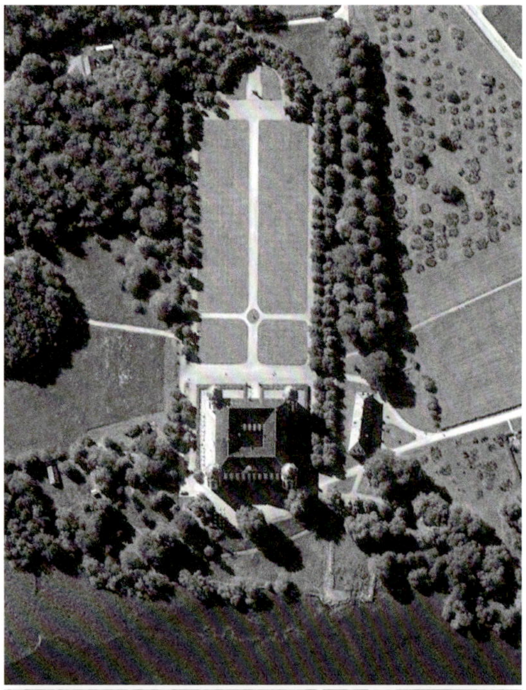

Skokloster Slott,
Skokloster, Sweden

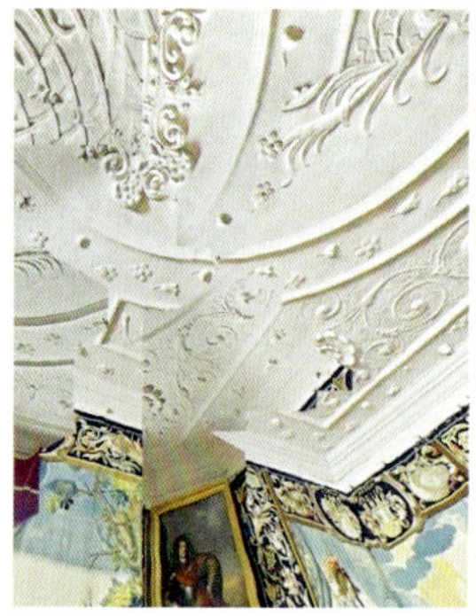

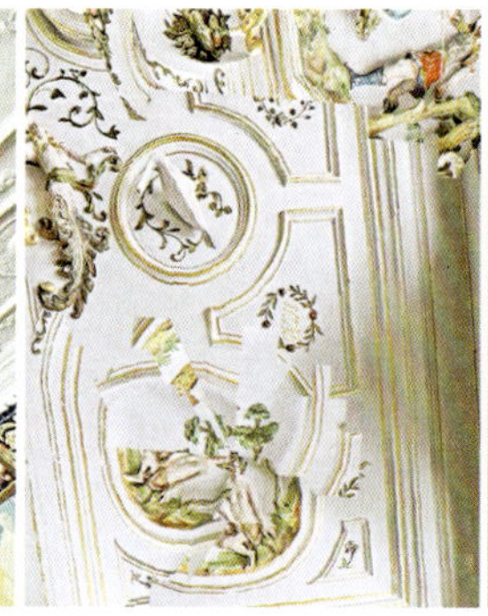

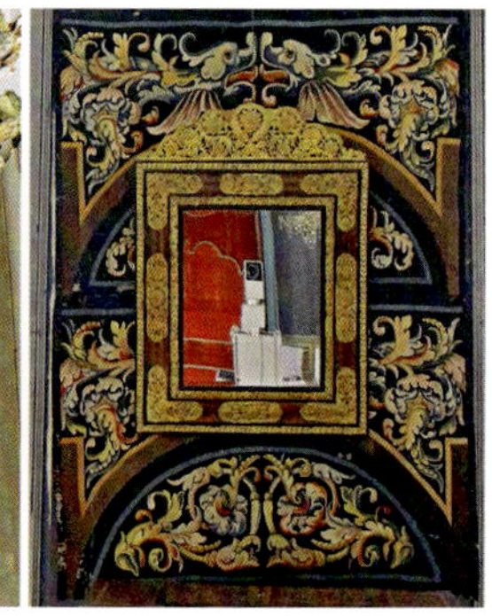

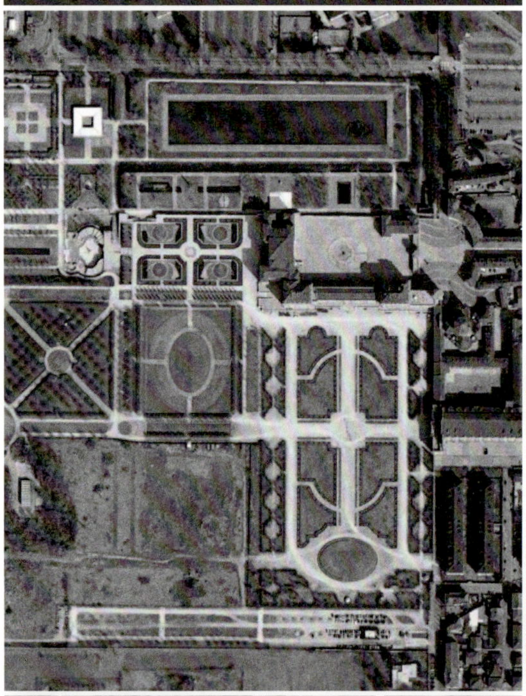

La Venaria Reale,
Venaria Reale, Italy

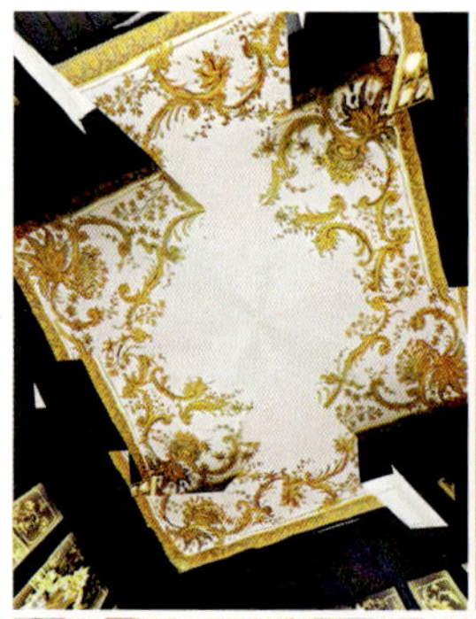

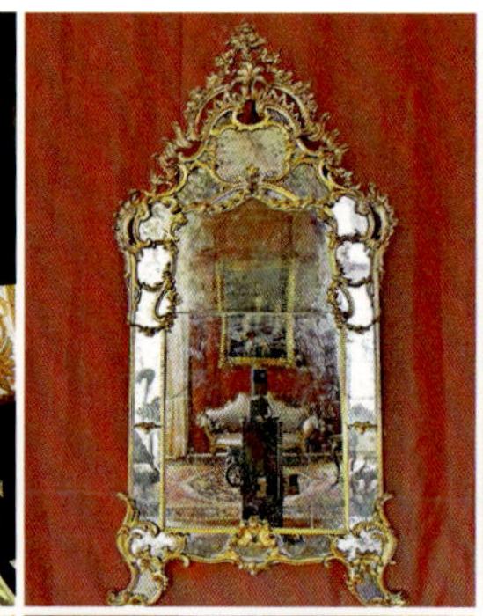

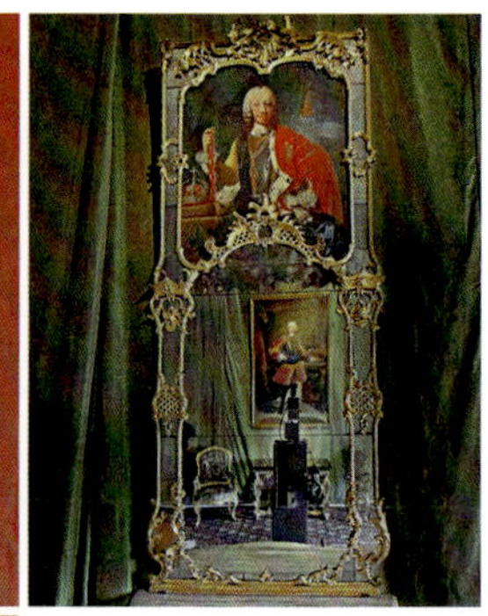

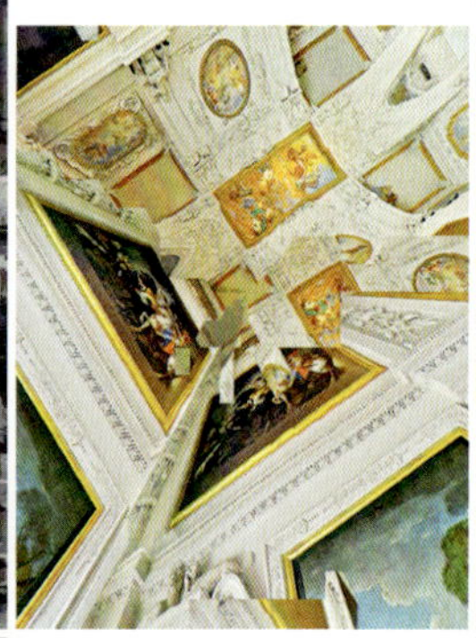

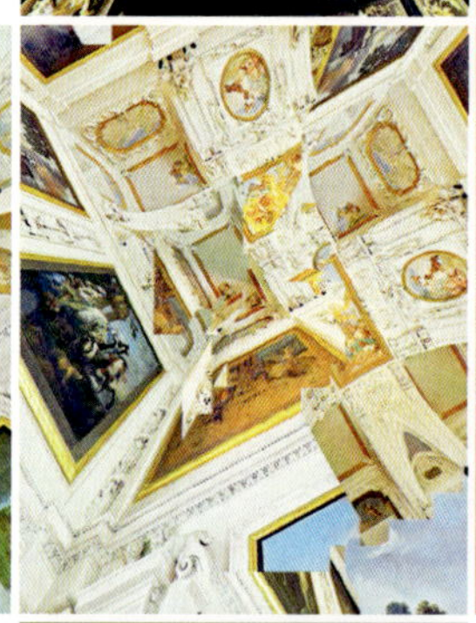

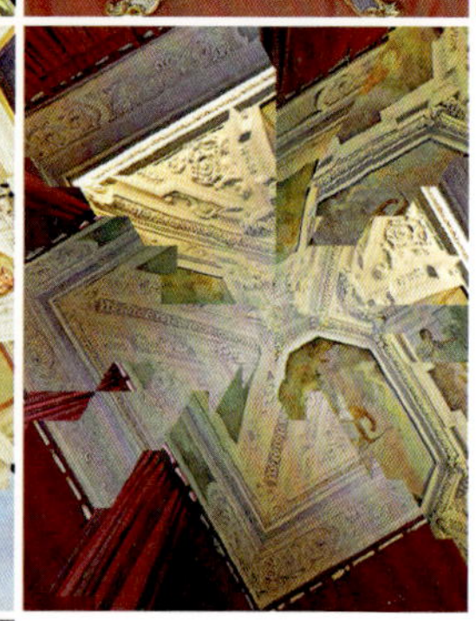

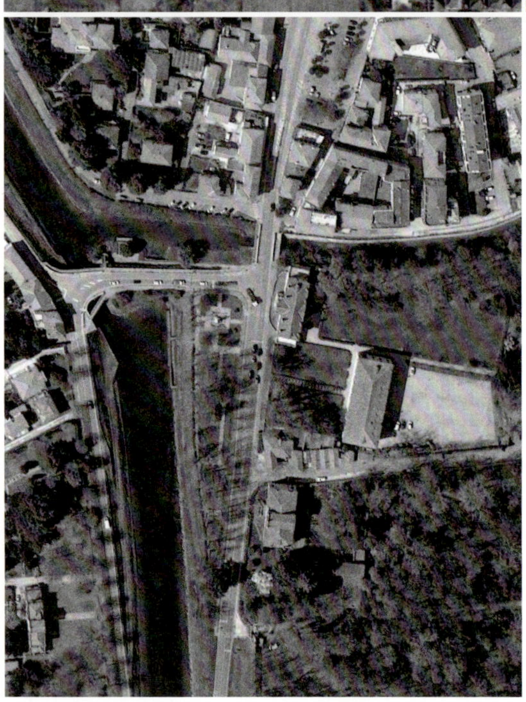

Villa Foscarini Rossi,
Stra, Italy

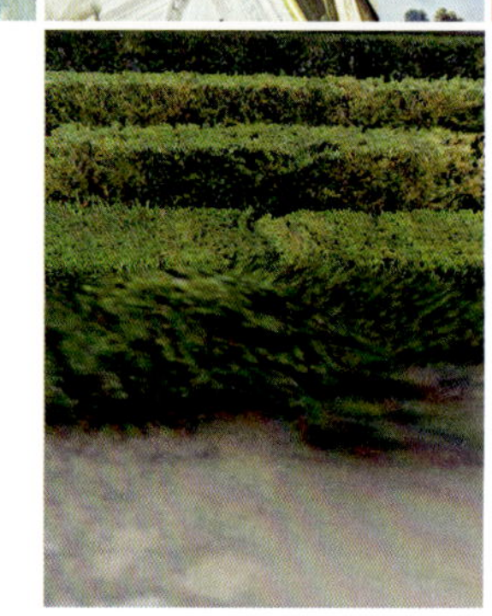

THERESA GANZ
GRAND ILLUSION

EDITED BY
Theresa Ganz and Joshua Chuang

TEXT BY
Joshua Chuang

COPY EDITOR
Lindsay Westbrook

PUBLISHING EDITOR
Agnese Cantelmi (Mousse)

DESIGN
Anna Azzali (Mousse)

PUBLISHED AND DISTRIBUTED BY
Mousse Publishing – Contrappunto srl
via Pier Candido Decembrio 28,
20137, Milan–Italy

AVAILABLE THROUGH
Mousse Publishing, Milan
moussemagazine.it
DAP | Distributed Art Publishers, New York
artbook.com
Les presses du réel, Dijon
lespressesdureel.com
Antenne Books, London
antennebooks.com
Idea Books, Amsterdam
ideabooks.nl
Motto, Berlin
mottodistribution.com
LibroCo, Firenze
libroco.it

PRINTED IN ITALY BY Artigiana Grafica

FIRST EDITION 2023

€ 18 / $ 22
ISBN 978-88-6749-607-5

ACKNOWLEDGEMENTS
To the memory of my grandparents and other elders, whose faith in culture, in spite of the traumas of the past, inhabited my thoughts as I made this work.

I want to acknowledge the influence of Peter York's essay "Trump's Dictator Chic" in Politico from March/April 2017. I had already been making these screenshots for over a year when I read it, but his essay clarified my vision.

Thank you to my parents Bob and Beth Ganz, my siblings Sarah Ganz Blythe and John Ganz and my husband Aneece Colt for reading and editing and encouraging and critiquing. Thanks also to my critique (support) group Meghann Riepenhoff and Stephanie Lindsay. Thank you to Joshua Chuang for hanging tough. Thank you to Anna Azzali and Agnese Cantelmi at Mousse, it's been a joy. Thank you also to Sie Ji Loo and Kristien Dodd at Brown for all your assistance.

This project has been made possible, in part, by the Brown Arts Institute, the Brown Faculty Development Fund, the Salomon Award and the Rhode Island Council on the Arts Fellowship Award.